PHILANTHROPY IN THE HISTORY OF AMERICAN HIGHER EDUCATION

PHILANTHROPY IN THE HISTORY OF AMERICAN HIGHER EDUCATION

Jesse Brundage Sears

www.General-Books.net

Publication Data:

Title: Philanthropy in the History of American Higher Education
Author: Sears, Jesse Brundage, 1876-
Publisher: Washington : Govt. Printing Office
Publication date: 1922
Subjects: Endowment of research – United States History
Endowments – United States History
Universities and colleges – United States Finance History

How We Made This Book for You
We made this book exclusively for you using patented Print on Demand technology.
First we scanned the original rare book using a robot which automatically flipped and photographed each page.
We automated the typing, proof reading and design of this book using Optical Character Recognition (OCR) software on the scanned copy. That let us keep your cost as low as possible.
If a book is very old, worn and the type is faded, this can result in typos or missing text. This is also why our books don't have illustrations; the OCR software can't distinguish between an illustration and a smudge.
We understand how annoying typos, missing text or illustrations, foot notes in the text or an index that doesn't work, can be. That's why we provide a free digital copy of most books exactly as they were originally published. Simply go to our website (www.general-books.net) to check availability. And we provide a free trial membership in our book club so you can get free copies of other editions or related books.
OCR is not a perfect solution but we feel it's more important to make books available for a low price than not at all. So we warn readers on our website and in the descriptions we provide to book sellers that our books don't have illustrations and may have typos or missing text. We also provide excerpts from each book to book sellers and on our website so you can preview the quality of the book before buying it.
If you would prefer that we manually type, proof read and design your book so that it's perfect, simply contact us for the cost. We would be happy to do as much work as you would be like to pay for.

1

PHILANTHROPY IN THE HISTORY OF AMERICAN HIGHER EDUCATION

This study represents an attempt to trace the influence of philanthropy in the development of higher education in America. Incident to this has beeu the further question of what has been evolved by way of a theory of educational endowments, or, broader still, of educational philanthropy. The importance of such a study is obvious when we consider the part philanthropy has played in the development of the American college and university. Its importance is equally clear, too, when we view the recent enormous increase in educational philanthropy, and the wide variety of educational enterprises to which philanthropy is giving rise. If we are to avoid the waste that must inevitably come from bad management of gifts, from wrong dispositions of money over which the future can exercise no control, we must study our already extensive experience and develop a set of guiding principles or a fundamental theory of educational philanthropy.

It was evident from the outset that any reasonably brief treatment of a subject occupying so large a place in the history of American higher education would present certain difficulties, not only In the selection of facts, but also in the interpretation of the comparatively small amount of first-hand data that could be satisfactorily treated in brief space.

It has been the writer's purpose carefully to scrutinize the materials presented to see that they were fully representative of one or another important type of philanthropy affecting our higher education; to see that no type of effort was without representation; to draw only such conclusions as the facts clearly warranted; and, finally, to present the data in such form as to make them fully available fur future use in more intensive studies, if occasion lor such should arise. If in these respects the effort has been successful, then it is believed to offer, in broad outline, the history of philanthropy in the development of American higher institutions of learning. As such it is presented, with the hope that it may add somewhat to the general perspective we now possess for the various features of our institutions for higher training, anil to the development of a sound theory of educational philanthropy, as well as with a full consciousness that there is very much yet to be done before we shall have adequate details concerning any one of the many phases of this problem.

At the beginning of our experience in this field Europe had formulated no theory of educational endowment or of educational philanthropy, hut subsequently the subject received treatment in the writings of their social ami political philosophers, and also to no less extent by practical statesmen engaged in correcting the evils of past mistakes in practice. These ideas have been traced briefly in an introductory chapter. Following this, it has been my purpose to describe our own practice from the beginning to the present time, and to make such generalizations as the facts seemed to warrant. Two types of data have been studied: First, the foundation documents, such as charters, articles f Incorporation, constitutions, by-laws, deeds of trust, v, and conditions controlling gifts on the one band; and. second, the sti of gifts "ii the other. To add to the value of bare description, the comparative method has been utilized wherever it was possible.

The writer is Indebted to numerous librarians and education boards Cor special courtesies, and especially bo Dr. Paul Monroe, not only for having ed tliis problem, but also for important suggestions concerning the method of its t reatment.

The original study of which this bulletin is a condensation is on file at Teachers College, Columbia University, where it was presented In April. L919, in partial fulfillment of the requirements tor the degree of doctor of philosophy, . I. B. Si LB i. Stanford University, Calif., April 20, 1919.

Chapter I.
DEVELOPMENT OF A THEORY OF PHILANTHROPY.
THE EARLY CONCEPTION OF PHILANTHROPY.
So long as charity remained intimately associated with the church it is not strange that the work it was doing should never have been called in question. The term "

charity" meant Christian virtue, and its economic significance was wholly overlooked. In praising a man's good intentions it was not thought Important that society should hold him responsible for having wisdom in expressing them. '

PLACE OF EDUCATIONAL FOUNDATIONS IN TURGOT's SOCIAL THEORY.

It is left, therefore, to the economist to look critically into the problem so long ignored by superstition, religion, and sentimentalism. It is interesting to note that it was in an age when all social life was being carefully scrutinized that Turgot published his unsigned article " Foundations," in the Encyclopedia, in 1757. It is at this point that a real halt is called, and philanthropy becomes a problem for the intellect.

All peoples and ages have regarded active benevolence as an important virtue, and to such acts the severest economist offers no protest. But the bald unwisdom evident in the presumption that man is competent to judge what is good for all the future is what drew from Turgot this classic criticism, which John Morley says is "the most masterly discussion we possess of the advantages and disadvantages of endowments."
1

The native instinct which underlies man's desire to relieve his brother in distress makes no distinction between present and future good; nor docs it discover that good is a relative term. Consequently, it is not strange that much evil is done where only good is intended. But add to this native impulse the best wisdom of our day and yet we can not say what will be the need of, another generation; and if we could, and were large-hearted enough to endow that need, we would not be able to guarantee that our successors, in whose 'John Morley: Diderot and the Encyclopaedists, p. 191.

nds we place the right, would execute with the same enthusiasm with which we have founded. Business, but aol enthusiasm, maj be banded down.

it is because the history of European endowments was written so plainly in these terms across the faces of the church, the hospital, and the school, thai Turgol was lead to Inquire Into the genera utility of foundations, with a view to demonstrating their impropriety. He does not approach the subject in a purely abstract way, though be had a well-defined social theory which later received a clear statement in his " Reflexions Bur la Formation et la Distribution des RIchesses," since tor every principle-et forth he appeals to history for its justlfication.

Turgol sees so little good accomplished by endowments that be is Led to say: " Un fondateur est un bomme qui veut terniser l'effel de ses volonte His motive may be good, but results prove his lack of wisdom. After citing cases which are convincing, he concludes: '. le oe craindrai point de 'lire- q si l'on comparait les advantages et les Inconvenients de toutes lea fondatio qui existent aujourd'hui en Europe, ii n'y en aurait peut-etre pas one qui soutinl L'examen d' une politique eclairfi."' Granting that at its conception the object is a real utility, there is yet the Impossibility of its future execution to be reckoned with, because the enthusiasm of the founder can not be trans rnitted. f even this, however, were overcome, it would still not be long till time would sweep away the utility, for society has not always the same needs.

'rims Turgot pointed out the difficulties and the consequent evils inherently connected with the establishment of perpetuities. If we suggest the idea of a periodica revision, which is done by later thinkers, Turgol quickly points to history and shows how long periods usually elapse after a foundation has become useless before Its uselessness Is detected; that those closelj acquainted with such a charity arc so accustomed to its working as not to In' struck by delect– and that those not acquainted have little chance of observing Its weakness. Then there is the difficulty of determining the proper character and extent of the modifications, to say nothing of enforcing its adoption against the opposition of the vested interests.

The author distinguishes two kinds of social needs which are intended to he fulfilled by foundations: ne. "appartlennent a la aocite entiere, el ne Beront que le resultant des in terete de chacunu de panic-,: tela Bont lea besoina i.-111 de r humanlte, la uourriture pour tons les hommes, lea bonnes moeura ei r education des enfants, pour toutes lea families; et eel h t est pins ou moine preasant pour les diffcrents besoina; car un bomme sent plus rlvement le besoin de la nourrlture que l' Int6rel qu'il a de donner A aea enfants une bonne education."' This need, be Bays, can not be fulfilled bj a foundation or nn.-on of gratuitous means, for the general g 1 must result from the efforts each individual in behulf of his own Interests, it is the business of the i. to rlestroj obstacles winch Impede man in in Industrj or in the enjoj men I ol it- frutta. Blmllarly, he insist that everj famllj owe- to its children an education, and that oulj through these individual efforts can the eral perfection of education arise it Interest in education is lacking, be would nrou e It bj meana of a system of pri i I;! on rnerll

Th.-i. oinl eln- of public i Is he would propose to meet bj foundations i ha classed i Identnl, limited in place ami time, having less to do with .-.! m of admlnl trntlon, ami thai may demand particular relief, Buch, p. I Instai lipporl of some old men. the hardship ol ' Ity, Of all . i I, p 300, 4 It 1.1.; epidemic, etc. For the amelioration of such needs he would employ the puhli revenues of the community, some contribution of all its members, and voluntary subscriptions from generous citizens. This scheme he declares to be not only efficient but impossible of abuse, for the moment funds are diverted from their proper use their source will at once dry up. This puts no money into luxury or useless buildings, it would withdraw no funds from general circulation, and place no land in idle hands. He points to the success of such associations in England, Scotland, and Ireland, and thus supports his theory with reference to present practice.

By these lines of thought he justifies the proposition that government has a right to dispose of old foundations. " L'utilite publique est la loi suprem," " he says, and adds that a superstitious regard for the intention of the founder ought not to nullify it.

These are the principles, not deduced from an imaginary law of nature alone, but carefully supported and justified at each point by the clear facts of history. All foundations are condemned by Turgot as worse than useless and his laissez fa ire doctrine would forbid the establishment of others. This was a bold doctrine to preach in the middle of the eighteenth century, but its impress was felt throughout Europe, and it is only a few decades till another member of the same school of economists lends support to these views.

PLACE OF EDUCATIONAL FOUNDATIONS IN ADAM SMITH'S FIIEE-TRADE ECONOMY.

Adam Smith's " Wealth of Nations," first published in 1770, tends to substantiate all Turgot had taught and to show that it applies particularly to educational endowments.

In discussing the natural inequalities of labor and stock, he insists that where there is "perfect liberty" all advantages and disadvantages tend to equality. 6 And in the following chapter on political inequalities of wages and profit he points out three ways in which political interference with " perfect liberty " has produced great and important inequalities. " First. by restraining the competition in some employments to a smaller number than would otherwise be disposed to enter into them; secondly, by increasing it in others beyond what it naturally would be; and thirdly, by obstructing the free circulation of labor and stock, both from employment to employment ami from pkye to place." ' In support of the second he shows how public money, "and sometimes the piety of private founders," 8 have drawn many people into the profession of the clergy, thereby increasing competition to the point of making the salaries very low. Exactly the same thing, he says, has happened to men of letters and to teachers, and when contrasted with the time of Isocrates. " before any charities of this kind had been established for the education of indigent people to the learned professions," the ill effect upon the teacher's income is evident enough.

There is yet another phase of the subject which is touched upon in Smith's discussion of the expense of the institutions for the education of the youth. Referring to the many endowed schools throughout Europe, he asks:

Have those public endowments contributed in general to promote the end of their institution? Have "they contributed to encourage the diligence and to improve the abilities of the teachers? Have they directed the course of education toward objects more useful, both to the individual and to the public, than those to which it would naturally have gone of its own accord? '"

5 TuikOt-Oeuvres, Vol. I, p. 308.

Smith, Adam: Wealth of Nations, Bk. I, Ch. X, p. 101.

7 Ibid., p. 121.

Ibid., p. 131.

Ibid., p. 134.

10 Ibid., p. 249.

He then states as a universal principle that the exertion of most people In a profession is proportional to the necessity they are under of making that ea ertioil He believes that the endowments of schools have diminished the nea sitj of application in the teachers, and shows how the older and richer oil. hare clung longesl to a useless and worn-out curriculum, while the poorer universities, dependent upon their popularity t'r much i' their income, Introduced the modern subjects much earlier." Be-ays:

Were there no public Institutions for education, no systems, no would be taughl for which there was not some demand, or which the circumstances of the times did not render it either necessarj or convenient, or at least fashionable, to learn. 11

This extreme application of the principle of free trade is modified only slightly by Smith t meet the inequality of opportunity brought aboul In a complex society where division of laimr has been carried to great Length. While he states that in most cases the state of society places the greater number of Individuals In such situations as form in them almost all the abilities and virtues which that state requires, yet there are cases In which this La not true.

The uciii whose whole life is spent in performing a few simple operation which tin- effects, too, are perhaps always the same, or very nearly the same, has no occasion t exerl his understanding or in exercise his invention in finding nut expedients fur remosin (litiicuities which never occur. He naturallj loses, therefore, the habil of such exertion, and generally becomes as stupid and Igno rant as it is possible for a human creature ti become. 11

Thus Smith would have the state intervene in behalf of the great labor population, Whose intellectual tendency must inevitably be in this direction.

This brief presentation Of Smith's attitude toward perpetuities BhoWS how his principles u BOCial Organization exclude them; and. like TUTgot'B, his theorj Is constructed in the presence of existing facts. The sum of the contribution is little mi. re than a specific application of Turgot's arguments t' educational foundationa If the social theory underlying the objections t" endowments made b tl two 1. en i sound, surelj the tacts thej have cited would warrant their eon elusion that endowments are evil because they interfere with the real laws uf human pre Certainly the evidence liny ne make-, clear the d lli. ill ties attending their establishment.

is a iai-. fain- policy a si. nnd basis fur social organization, and can these 1 practices be overcome? These are problems for then- suc. e-s. irs.

Will. I. M. 'N 111 m Bi 'i in 'a 1 in 1 R1.

William von Humboldt wrote, in 1791: "Ueberhaupl s,. n die Erzlehung nur, ohne Rill slchl auf bestluuute, den Menschen zu erthellende btirgerlii Formen,

Men hen bilden; bedari ee ir Staata nicht." M Thus he doi oulj accepts the system. f free exchange laid down bj 1 urgol ami Smith, bul excludes the possible modification which Turgol implies under the head of "accidental"

:, n. i which Smith makee i" correct the sllghl disadvantage t which seme are pher, i bj the "i' the extreme division oi labor. " 1 a en Men chen gewunen a lie Oewerbe beaaren Fortgang; bluhen alle Km, te .,,,,., B uf 1 e rw(oh alle lasenachaften," saj- v llliam von Humboldt,

"Tic- . iltta (N Bfc. 'ii 1. 1

"bid., p, 2(win., in. rod Bumboldt, Work, Vol VII, p 57, and again, "Bei freuen Menschen entsteht Xachoiivrung, and es bildea sich bessere Erzieher wo ihr Schiksal von dem Erfolg Ihrer Arbeiten, als wo es on dor Beforderung abhangt, die sie vom Staate zu erwarten baben."

Hero we find a loading German statesman insisting upon these social and economic principles in matters of education. Surely he did not foresee the future development of schools in Germany, where the State lias boon responsible for practically all edu- cational work.

While our purpose here is not to write, or even to sketch, the history of economic theory, yet it is interesting to note that the objections soon to be raised against a wholesale condemnation of educational endowments are focused upon the economic doctrine of the physiocrats, and tit in as early steps in the historical decline of the laissez faire economy.

Chalmers's modification of the earlier theories.

Dr. Thomas Chalmers, an early nineteenth century economist, interested in the practical problem of handling the poor, accepts the idea of free exchange to the extent of condemning the state endowment of pauperism but urges that an endowment for the relief of indigence is not to be compared with one whose object is the support of literary or Christian instruction. For education, though it is a real want, is not a felt want. He says:

The two cases, so far from being at all alike in principles, stand in direct and diametric opposition to each other. We desiderate the latter endowment because of the languor of the intellectual or spiritual appetency; in so much that men, left to themselves, seldom or never originate a movement toward learning. We deprecate the former endowment because, in the strength of tile physical appetency, we have the surest guarantee that men will do their uttermost for good; and a public charity having this for its object by lessening the industry and forethought that would have been otherwise put forth in the cause, both adds to the wants and detracts from the real work and virtue of the species. And, besides, there is no such strength of compassion for the sufferings of the moral or spiritual that there is for the physical destitution. An endowment for education may be necessary to supplement the one, while an endowment for charity may do the greatest moral and economic mischief by superseding the other. Relatives and neighbors could bear to see a man ignorant or even vicious. They could not bear to see him starve. 15

Thus an important modification of the above social theory is proposed. Whether the practical philanthropist has since shown such discrimination or not, the principle involved in the criticism was important. Shall the provision for education be dependent upon the mere demand of the market, or shall this important but " unfelt " need be stimulated by some kind of endowment?

mill's opposition to the theories of turgot and smith.

In February. 1833, John Stuart Mill published an article in the Jurist " in which he declared ignorance and want of culture to be the sources of all social evil, and adds that they can not be met by political checks." He says:

There is also an unfortunate peculiarity attending these evils. Of all calamities, they are those of which the persons suffering from them are apt to be least aware. Of their bodily wants and ailments, mankind are generally cons: ions; but the wants of the mind, the want of being wiser and hotter, is. in the far greater number of cases, unfelt; some of its disastrous consequences are felt, but are ascribed to any imaginable cause except the true one. 15 lb Quoted by Thos. Mackay in " The State and Charity," p. 36.

10 Later published in " Dissertations and Discussions," Vol. I, pp. 28-68.

17 Mill, J. S.: " Dissertations and Discussions," Vol. I, p. 54.

18 Ibid., pp. 54, 55.

G PHILAX. HKnpy A. MI. KKAX HIGHER EDUCATION.

In answer t" the question as to what oven have depended upon and must depend upon for the removal of their Ignorance and defects of culture, he says, mainly on the unremitting exertions of tl more Instructed and cultivated," which, in- adds, is a wide field! usefulness open fox foundations. He eom-bats Smith's argument that such foundations are but premiums on Idlem and Lnsufficiencj merely t. y saying that sin-h is the case onlj when it is nobody's business to see that the trust is. inly executed.

Tn show further how the Idea of endowments fits into Mill's general social philosophy, not." what he says in his essay " n Liberty," written in is.". s:

With regard to the merely contingent, or, as it may he called, constructive injury which a person causes to society, by conduct which neither violates any specific duty to the public, nor occasions perceptible hurt to anj assignable individual except himself, the Inconvenience is one which society can afford to hear, for the sake of the greater good of human freedom."

Individual freedom is as carefully guarded as by Turgol or Smith, but the implication that it is best preserved by a complete Bystem of free exchange La carefully avoided.

Mill does not believe that in a government where majority rule predominates the ideas of the minority should he lost, in his essay on M Endowments," published in the Fortnightly Review, April l, I860, he says:

There is good reason against allowing them to do this I make bequests) in favor Of an tinhorn individual whom they can not know, or a public purpose beyond the probable limits of human foresight Bui within those limits, the more scope thai Is given to varieties of human individuality the hotter.

And,

Since trial alone can decide whether any particular experiment Is successful, latitude should be;: iven for carrying on ih experiment until the trial is complete."

His ontentlon is, then, nol only thai foundations should be permitted, but thai over a reasonable period of time the exact wishes of the founder should strictly adhered to. His defense, later In the essay, of a foundation just then being severely criticized by the press shows the greal social import which he attai I e to the preservation of an unusual idea of an unusual person. After a complete trial of the experiment has been effected, the obligation of to the founder has been discharged, and the value of the glfl to society can he Indicated.

The explanation of thi relationship Is the firsl object of ti Bsaj of i v ':::.

the mh ond being a discussion of the Bplril In which and the reservations w th which the legislature should proceed to accept and i liry ti Iglnal plan unil objeel ol the foundation, in brief, he regards the endowment as public property after about fifty years from the date of its establishment, and in everj ubjecl to the will of odety, even to changing the purpose of the-ift. iti o meet tbe i ban es ol

Mill's economic justification ol man' righl to h endowments Is quite a h ting b in oclal justification. He Bays that it i– due not to the children bul to the parents thai the) Bhould have the power ol bestowing their i, according to t hen- own preference and Judgment, for p. i f the attributes of property; ti wnershlp of a ti not be looked upon as complete without the power of bestowing it. al death or

On i. ii" rty," published In the Harvard i on " The i;. la ind Wroi h Interference itti Corj l b F i. In D during: life, at the owner's pleasure; and all the reasons which recommend that private property should exist recommend pro tanto extension of it. 21

This is no small-modification of the theories of Turgot and Smith, and le a definite stand taken by Mill in respect not only to a philosophical but to an important practical issue then before the English public. And only a few years before his death he wrote in his autobiography" that the position he had taken in 1833 was as clear as he could now make it. Indeed, this very principle of Mill's was in 1853 embodied in the legislative enactment carried through by Lord Brougham and others.

mr. lowe's return to free trade principles.

Mill's position, however, was too conservative, and too considerate of the numerous abuses of endowments then so well known to everyone, and drew forth sharp criticisms. 23 In condemning the report of the commissioners appointed to inquire into middle-class education, whose procedure had been generally in line with the ideas of Mill and Chalmers, Mr. Lowe" (later Lord Sherbrooke) calls for a return to the ordinary rules of political economy. He would class teaching as a trade, and keep it in the quickening atmosphere of free exchange. This return to the notion that failure of endowments is due not to founder worship, as Mill would say, but to the principle of endowment, shows the influence of the free-trade economy.

In practice at this time the cry is not that all foundations be used to pay the national debt, and so place education where Mr. Lowe would ask, but rather how can the terrible waste of funds be checked, or, what system of control can the State legitimately exercise? We have Mill's suggestion that society will progress most rapidly when it gives wide range to social and educational experimentation, and that this is done best, not by the State through a commission, which would tend to force all endowments into a uniform mold, but by legal enforcement of the exact conditions of the foundation till the merits of the experiment become evident.

HOBHOUSE ON " THE DEAD HAND " IN EDUCATION.

During the period 1868 to 1879 Sir Arthur Hobhouse delivered a series of addresses, afterwards published as " The Dead Hand," " in which he accepts, with Mill, both the principle of endowed education and the idea that every such bequest should be made to serve the present. The question of method. however, is a point on which he takes issue with Mill. He can not see that the term "property" implies power of posthumous disposition. Tried by history. he says, " the further back we trace any system of laws, the smaller we find the power of posthumous disposition to be." 20 Furthermore, he insists thai 250 years of English experience does not reveal one useful educational experiment resulting from such foundations as Mr. Mill regards Important in the development of new ideas and lines of social and educational practice."

21 Mill, J. S.: "Political Economy," Vol. I,-p. 287.

22 Autobiography, p. 182.

24 See Report of Schools Inquiry Commission of 1868.

84 See his Middle Class Education, Endowment or " Free Trade."

25 London, 1880.

Hobhouse, Sir A.: " The Dead Hand," p. 14. 27 Ibid., p. 94.

This attitude is further emphasized by sir Joshua I-"it-l 1. whose practical contact with English educational endowments gives weight to his words when he says:

One uniform purpose is manifest In the testaments, the deeds "f gift and the early statutes by which the character of these Bchools was Intended to be shaped. It is to encourage the pursuit of a liberal education founded on the ancient languages. 11

Further, In bis analysis of the motives which have prompted bequests t public uses. Hobhouse does not find justification for Mill's position. In the list of motives which he finds underlying the foundations In England arc: Love power and certain cognate passions, ostentatiousnees, vanity, superstition, patriotism to a slighl extent, and spite.-' 8 While this list mighl not lit Individual i ases, he insists that it Is true for the mass.

Mill thinks that the public l es not know its own needs fully, because it i,. ni the majority speaking. Hobhouse regards the public as at: Individual competent to judge its needs and naturally endowed with the right to expn them; hence he would lay down two principles upon which all foundations must he established: First, "If the public is chosen as Legatee, the Legacy shall he, as it ought to he. an unconditional one'"; and. second. " there shall alwa s he a living and reasonable owner of property, to manage it according to the wants of mankind."" The excuse for such a title to his 1 k here becomes evident lie can not see that the Living have need for the continual advice and control of the dead.

OTHER EN, I, Ism THEORIES.

Interest In education grew in England, respeel for perpetual trusts de creased. The act of 1853 above referred to, giving a commission power onlj to Inquire into and report the com i it ion of charitable foundations, was later revised giving the commission greater power. And finally, In 1869, one yen- after the report of the School nquiry Commission, we have the "Endowed schools act," " giving the commissioners powei to "render any educational endowment conducive to the advancement of the education of hoys and girls,"" etc. This acl was somewhat strengthened by revision In 1873 and again In L874

During the last half of the nineteenth century there was wide discussion of the practical problem In England, but little of theoretical value was added. Sir Joshua I'itfch, in an address at Pennsylvania Dniveralty," lays down two principles: First, an endowment's onlj right to exist Is its benefit to the community; and, second, the state is the supreme trustee of all endowments. Thomas Hare, in L869, 1 ' regards all property as either public or private. An endowment, lx public property, is subject to 'lie public win. Before the Social Science elation," he accepts Mill's notion of endowments as valuable social and educa tional experiments, and Insist onlj upon the state's righl of supervision.

-i m m i: v AND I 0N it HON.

1 niv other writer added bits of practical wisdom, but the result more than a hundred years of theorising maj be brieflj summed up as follows: i ltd Ed A '"i Methods," f- 191.

Hobl ' " The l ed Sand," p. LB If.

Fitch, Jo bua Bdocatloaej Ainu and Methods," p, L20, "Ibid. p. 121 " Bee " '-' nil, i it. i odowed s, let, IMS-' tad; ' Wet. I i7 Vict, i 11 let, C B7.

n Bducetionej Mme end Methods."- i oi tnlghtlj Rev, "Trea. so. Be. A m. r i eo, p. tax,

There is perhaps no universally acceptable theory of educational endowments yet worked out; the early free-trade economy luis been tempered by substantially removing education from its scope; the experimental value of the endowed school is accepted on the ground that social progress is dependent quite as much upon the ideas and interests of the minority as upon those of the majority, and that with wide variation in educational endeavor, opportunity for wise selection is increased; that endowments are public property, since they are given to public service, and should therefore be subject to such public supervision as will prevent their being wasted or becoming socially obnoxious.

Recalling Turgot's position, we can see that his statement of the meaning and function of foundations is yet a fairly acceptable presentation of the philosophical problem.

Chapter II. THE COLONIAL PERIOD.

INFLUENCES AFTECTING THE BEGINNING F AMERICAN IIKilli);

EDUCATION.

I. Tin; PROBLEM.

In early colonial America there was little theorizing as to who should build colleges or as to how such schools should be financed. From the beginning higher education was a serious Interest of the people, and one which rariy found practical expression. What the scholars and statesmen thought of endowments, therefore, we can infer only from what they actually did. They laced college building as a practical problem, and whatever we have since developed by way of a theory of endowed education in America we have developed very largely out of our long and varied experience.

In this and succeeding chapters, therefore, it is the purpose to assemble facts which will adequately describe thai experience, to the end thai the character and extenl of the Influence which philanthropy has had In the developmenl of higher education In America may be Been. Finally, from an Interpretation of these facts II should then be possible to state whatever theory of endowments there has been evolved In this country.

when in the early history of Harvard College we find among; t donors the general cunt, numerous towns and churches, as well as Individuals, we realize thai it Is uecessary to define the term "philanthropy." In this study the term is used to Include all gifts excepl those from state. Again, if. as we are told, philanthropy means an expression of love for mankind, the Dames of Bleazer Wheelock, Theodoras J. Frellnghuysen, Morgan Edward,. lames Blair, and other notable ministers of the gospel would loom large In the description. However important the work. i Buch men may have been, it would be Impossible satisfactoril) to–how Its results In a Btudy which designed to be quite largelj quantitative. Accordingly, this Btudj will be concerned with only those facts and forces which play some measurable part i itutlona of higher learning 2. COLLEGE CHABTEBS kltALYSED

The forcea which entered Into the founding of our Brat colleges were many

Certain of these si i out clearlj and for man years played ; i i directing the growth of higher learning Everywhere and particularly In the foundation documents of the colonial colleges we arc able to th at work, giving form to thea I Institutions In

Table i are mown such data, taken from the charters ol the nine colonial I olh.

English Influences are suggested by the three names, William and. Mary. King's, and Queen's. To these Dartmouth must he added, having taken its name in honor of its chief benefactor. Lord Dartmouth, of England, and. for a similar reason, Yale. Further, important subscriptions were collected in England: 10,000 for Dartmouth;. 4,500 for Brown; 2,500 for William and Mary in addition to the gift of the English Government of 2,000 and 20.000 acres of land; King's and Pennsylvania together, some 10,000;

and over 2,000 for Princeton. 2 In all cases these subscriptions furnished relatively large sums for the colleges, and were among the early, and in case of William and Mary, Dartmouth and Brown, the founding gifts.

AIM OF THE COLLEGES GIFTS EXPECTED.

Harvard University. " Through the good hand of God " men " are moved and stirred up to give for the advancement of all good literature, arts, and sciences."

"Many well-devoted persons have been and daily are moved and stirred up to give and bestow sundry gifts, legacies, lands, and revenues for the advancement of all good literature, arts, and sciences in Harvard College."

College of William and Mary. " That the Church of Virginia may be furnished with a seminary of ministers of the Gospel, and that the youth may be piously educated in good letters and manners and that the Christian faith may be propagated amongst the western Indians, to the glory of Almighty God; to make a place of universal study, or perpetual college of divinity, philosophy, languages, and other good arts and sciences.

Yale University. To found a school " Wherein Youth may be instructed in the Arts and Sciences, who through the blessings of Almighty God may be fitted for Public employment both in Church and Civil State."

"Several men have expressed by Petition their earnest desires that full Liberty and Privilege be granted unto certain Undertakers for the founding, suitably endowing and ordering a Collegiate School," etc., also note further the power given to the trustees of the college.

Princeton University. "For the instruction of youth in the learned languages and in the liberal arts and sciences." All religious sects to have equal educational opportunity. 4

Columbia University. "For Instruction and Education of Youth in the Learned Languages and in the Liberal Arts and Sciences." "to lead them from the Study of Nature, to the Knowledge of themselves, and of the God of Nature, and their Duty to Him."

University of Pennsylvania. The academy out of which the College grew was "for instructing youth for reward, as poor children on charity" "we, being desirous to encourage such pious, useful, and charitable designs." College is for instruction "in any kind of literature, arts, and sciences."

1 Pennsylvania University Bulletin, Vol. Ill, p. 4, January. 1899, contains n copy of the "Fiat" for the Royal Brief, issued by King George III, granting the righl to the two " Seminaries" to take the subscription.

2 See Maclean: History of the College of New Jersey, Vol. r. 147 ff. for a discussion of this undertaking; also copies of some documents connected with it. The full amount of the subscription is not known.

8 Charter was not granted till 16."i0. " New England's First Fruits" shows clearly the religious aim. Also the legislative act of 1642 uses the words piety, morality, and learning as expressing the aim of the college.

' See Princeton Univ. Catalogue, 1912-13, p. 46. The quotation is not from the charter, the first charter not being extant, but is from an advertisement in the Pennsylvania Gazette of Aug. 13, 1746-47. Nearly the same words are used in the charter of 1S0O to express the aim of the college. 111512 22 5 =–g

SS9o. a, S a W S .-.- ! o c 3.3: c- c c ' =
Sill bjjgf M h a 03-3.2 S"-d
M ftco - d 05.2 3 ft 'fed o23-2S 2,33 .5-2
SowSxa'Sg'sqq
S 6 tr.2 Q boo–" 3 jpjj =.2S2 otcb p ft g"d
"S owSw ."CO 6t0= - c7oc" (sra? Wdw 03S-Bts

"Several benevolent and charitable persons have generously paid, and by subscriptions promised hereafter to pay, for the use of said acini emy, divers sums of money," spent " in maintaining an academy there as well for the instruction of poor children on charity," etc." 1

Brown University.- "And whereas a Public School or Seminary, to which the South may freely resort for Education In tin- vernacular and learned Languages, and in the liberal Arts ami Sciences would be for the u'en-eral Advantage and Honor of the Government,"

And whereas Daniel Jenckes, Esq.; with manj others appear as undertakers in the valuable Design praying thai full Liberty and Power may be granted unto such of them, to found, endow, a College," etc. And, further, "Being willing t encourage such an honorable and useful Institution, We, the said Governor," etc.

Rutgers College. The college is for "the Education of youth in the learned languages, libera and useful arts and BCiences, and especially in divinity." Did it try to preserve the hutch language? 1

Dartmouth College. "Dartmouth College, for the education and instruction of Youth the Indian Triios in Learning necessary for civilizing and christianizing Pagans in Arts and Sciences; also of English Youth."

it hath been represented that the Reverend Eleazer Wheelocs did, at his own expense, set on fool an Indian Charity school and for several years through the assistance of well-disposed Persons," etc."

3. RELIGIOUS AM) DENOMINATIONAL INFLUENCES.

The religious influence is. of course, prominent. The statements Bbowing bow the movements for establishing the schools were Btarted, those showing the source of control, the n't i ioners for the charters, and the religious affiliations of the first presidents, as well as the last one. showing the aim of the college, ail point to religion as the large motivating force in the case of everj olie.

The beginning of William ami Mary. Yale, Princeton, King's, Brown, Queen's, and Dartmouth (Harvard si id probably be Included) lies with groups of mini ter or religious bodies. In the case of Yale, Princeton, Brown, Queen's, and Dartmouth the formal request for b charter was presented bj represenl atives of religious bodies; while the source of control in the case ot Yale. King's, ami Brown was placed in the hands of religious bodies, in effect the: is true of Princeton, Harvard, and Queen's All the first presidents were mlnlsb l is in the charter, however, that the religloUS motive stands OUt with greatest prominence. The quotations presented are those which seem best to reveal tie chief aim of the Institution. Somewhere In everj charter, Pens le exception, there is evidence that the! e; ic in,, I' relk'ioil uas to he a prom neni feature of I he u,, rk "I' the colli I

Acad In catalogue, 191 IB Thli Ii of count tt" f the ter for n col.! two rean Istei i ii
'. i 1912-18, pp 29 80 Ifnrraj "Hint of Kduc m n i," Bfi refoi to the charter of 1770 as
amend iiik; i rtatemenl which. 6 V been Included In the Brat charter, rhr thai the i nit.
ii langaagi wrae to he iaed esdneivelj la tl luece.

ari-r. ii. iii i of Dartmouth College and Hj rer, N n. p 042.

To what extent denominationalism was a factor does not appear fully from this
table. From other sources we know that the chancellorship of William and Mary
was by charter granted to the Bishop of London; that Vale, which was built by
Congregationalists in a Congregational colony, said in her charter that at least the
major part of their 10 self-perpetuating trustees must always "be ministers of the Gospel
inhabiting within this colony." 1 ' Princeton's Charter, does not call for denominational
control, yet, according to the charter i 1648, there were 12 Presbyterian ministers on
the board. 10 It is also true that Governor Morris, of New Jersey, refused Princeton's
first request for a (baiter made, in his opinion, by a body of dissenters."

These, as well as the connection which the schism in the Presbyterian Church in
1741-1745 had with the beginning of Princeton," are evidence enough that denominationalism, if not even sectarianism, was a factor in its early life. In King's College
about two-thirds of the 41 trustees were members of the Church of England, though
they were not chosen officially upon religious grounds. The Pennsylvania College is
an exception, for its charter shows its aim to have been broadly human, though not
specifically religious, and certainly not denominational. By Brown's charter, however, 22 of her 36 trustees must be Baptists. There are no statements in the charters
of Queen's and Dartmouth that they are to be controlled by certain religious sects,
yet there is no doubt that the Dutch Reformed Church controlled Queen's and that
Dartmouth was nonsectarian, but with half the board of trustees constituted of ministers, 13 the whole enterprise being threatened when the Reverend Wheelock refused
to accept Governor Wentworth's proposal to make the Bishop of London an ex officio
member of the board of trustees. 14 It is noticeable, too, that the formal request for
the charter of Yale was made by a group of Congregational clergy, that of Princeton
by Presbyterian clergy, that of Brown by the Philadelphia Baptist Association, and
that of Queen's by the clergy and congregations of the Dutch Reformed Church.

The first president of Harvard was of Puritan training, and later was forced to resign
because he agreed with the Anabaptists on the subject of infant baptism." The first
president of King's was a minister of the Church of England, and the inclusion of this
requirement in the charter caused bitter opposition to the granting of the charter, a
bitterness healed only by the addition of a professor of divinity "To be chosen by the
Consistory of the (Dutch) Church for the time being." 1 The first rector (president) of
Yale was a Congregational minister. Brown's first president was a Baptist minister,
and Queen's a minister of the Dutch Church.

POLITICAL INFLUENCE.

The political influence is evident enough. Harvard was established by the colonial
government. William and Mary was founded by the English and Virginia Governments, and Kings by the New York Legislature. Yale's charter

Charter of the Collegiate School (Yale College) Catalogue, 1912-13, p. 64.

10 Maclean: " History of the College of New Jersey," Vol. I, 92.

11 Ibid., p. 34.

12 Ibid., p. 24.

"Charter, in Chase, P., "History of Dartmouth College and Hanover, N. H., Vol. I. 642 14 Letter of Wheelock to Gov. Wentworth, of New Hampshire. See History of Lhirt mouth College and Hanover, N. H., by F. Chase, p. 115 ff.

16 Pierce, Benjamin: "Hist, of Harvard Univ. from its Foundation, in the year 1636, to the Period of the Amer. Rev.," p. 10.

18 Fulton, John. "Memoirs of Frederick A. P. Barnard," p. 3ir ' ff. See also Bcclel-astical records of the State of New York.

- the youth: ir." to t- Instructed to the end thai "they may be fitted for public employment both in the church and civil state." and her Brat oionej gift was 120 country pay from the colony.

That these colleges were Intended from the beginning to rest upon gifts of the people is suggested In the quotations from the charters riv-ri above. If nol so stated, then the tad that the charter is granted to a body f men seeking to establish a college, together with the absence of any evidence that the state was accepting the responsibility, makes the Inference clear. It is to be noted, too. that Harvard. Yah', Brown. Kutu'ors, and Dartmouth received their names from their tirst great benefactors, and that In only three cases were the tirst funds of the college granted hy the legislatures.

To seek further evidence that the colonial colleges were or were not State institutions is not our present purpose. There is evidence here to show that the principle of state aid to higher education is as old as Harvard College. Yd the movement for each of the colleges, possibly excepting Harvard, was initiated either by a single man with great missionary zeal, or by a group of men, and not h the state.

From this preliminary examination of these foundation documents, then, one gathers some notion of the setting which our problem is t have, Judged by the facts presented, as well as in terms of the hard wort associated with the starting of these Institutions, philanthropy Is clearlj the mother of the colonial colleges.

FINANCES OF THE EARLY COLLEGES.

1. SCARCITY OF MONKY.

Down to 1693 we had but one college, that founded at Cambridge in u;:'.". Then- is probablj nowhere available to-day a complete record of all the early gifts to Harvard, but whal have been brought together lure will doubtless give a fairly satisfactory exhibit of the nature and extent of the earliest philanthropy devoted to higher education in this country.

There is one thing so characteristic of the early gifts to all the colonial colleges that it must receive brief notice at the outset Thai La, the size and kind of gifts. Harvard records the receipl "of a Dumber of sheep bequeathed by one man, of a quantity of cotton cloth, worth: i shillings, presented bj another. of a pewter flagon, worth 10 shillings, by a third, of a frull dish, a Bugar spoon, a silver tipt Jug, ne great salt, and one suiull treciirr so i by others." i rom

Vaie' earls blstorj the sentiment attaching to the words: " I give those i lea for founding a college in Connecticut," pronounced by each of the trustees aa he placed his little contribution upon the table, could not be Bpared, and bel it charter had been granted a formal gift of the "glass and nails which should be necessary to erecl a college and hall" had been made, I Wheelock, the founder and Hrsl president of Dartmouth, In a letter replying to criticisms ol the " plainness of the surroundings" al the college, says: " As to the coll it owns hut one (tablecloth), thai was lately given i. a generous lady in Con oecticut, and of ber own manufacture." " and again la a letter to the Honorable ommli loner for Indian Affairs, etc., he Bays, after Indicating the impossible financial condition in which the college finds Itself: " I have, v iih the assistance i number of those who nave contributed then old pul off clothing, supported them (th(along hitherto."" Doubtless similar examples could be

Pelrei 11 I of Harvard Univ., p it.

. if r i i ollegc Barnars'i Jour. f EDtfa V, 042 U I,,! in Chase's Hist, if i uruni uui Collage sod Haaovw, v it.

Ibuj.,.

taken from the subscription lists that yielded relatively large amounts bo Princeton, Queen's, Brown, and William and. Mary if these were extant.

In these gifts there is reflected much of the simplicity of the social and eco nomic life of that time. Actual money was scarce, as shown by the repeated issues of currency by the various Colonies, hence such gifts as Dartmouth's sawmills and blacksmith shop and Harvard's printing press entered most naturally and effectively into the making of colleges in those days.

2. USE OF THE SUBSCRIPTION METHOD.

These colleges were all active in gathering funds by the subscription plan both in England and in America. Princeton received a subscription of 1,000 proclamation, given in produce and money, in the southern Colonies in 1769, another of 1,000 from Boston in the same year, and 2,000 in England. Brown received 4,500 by subscription in England and Ireland in 1764." Blair brought home from England 2,500 which he had gathered by subscription for William and Mary in 1693. Dartmouth collected 10,000 in England in 1769, while King's and Pennsylvania shared equally a subscription fund of 10,000 gathered in England. These are only the most striking instances of the use of this method of collecting the gifts of the people. Through the churches this method was repeatedly used and frequently the colonial court or the town officials would name a day on which a subscription for the college would be asked from every citizen.

3. FEW LARGE GIFTS.

In that day of small gifts a few names of great benefactors stand out. Whatever the " moiety " of Harvard's estate was, it was a princely sum in the year 163S for a college with one or two teachers and a half dozen students." This was the first great gift to education in America, and it is worthy of note that it was not tied up with conditions which might make it useless to the Harvard College of the future. It was given by request to the college outright, and constituted half of the fortune and the entire library of one of the wealthiest and most noted men in New England.

The immediate influence of this was great, and is well recorded by the historians of the college, Quincy and Peirce. During the next few decades several gifts of 100 were received, and in 1650 Richard Saltonstall, of England, gave "to the college" goods and money worth 320 pounds sterling. In 1681 Sir Matthew Holworthy bequeathed " to be disposed of by the directors as they shall judge best for the promotion of learning and promulgation of the Gospel " 1,000. The Hon. William Stoughton erected a building in 1699 which cost 1,000 Massachusetts currency. These are the large gifts of the seventeenth century, with the exception of the gift of William and Mary, of England, to the college of Virginia.

During the next century Thomas Hollis established a professorship of divinity at Harvard (1721). In his- "orders"" he asks "that the interest of the funds be used, 10 annually for help to a needy student for the ministry a- many of these as the funds will bear." He reserves the right to sanction all appointments during his lifetime, then leaves it to the "President and Fellows at Harvard College," and asks "that none be refused on account of his belief and 21 Names of the first subscribers are given in the Collections of the Kbode Island Bis torical Society, Vol. VII, 273.

22 A careful discussion of the amount of this legacy is given in Quincy's History of Harvard, Vol. I, appendix I, 460.

28 See Quincy's Harvard, Vol. I, Appendix XLII, for copy of the instrument of gift.

practice of adult baptism."" The conditions which he places upon this, the first professorship established In America by private donation, are of interest. These are his words; I order and appoint a Professor of Divinity, to read lectures in the Hall of the College unto the students; the said Professor i" be Dominated and appointed from time to time by the President ami Pel lows of Harvard Coll and that the Treasurer pay to him forty pounds per aunum for his service, and that when choice is made of a fitting person, to lit recommended to me for my approbation, if I ie yet living."

in that day of fierce theological controversies these Beem to be very liberal conditions.

a few years later Hoiiis established a professorship of mathematics and natural philosophy. In all. his donations total over 5,000, a sum which far exceeded any single gift to education in America up to that time. Aside from hooks and goods the purposes of all his gifts were stipulated, but in smh general terms and, as his letters show," so fully in terms of the wishes of (he president and overseers, thai it constitutes an example of educational philanthropy t hal is worthy of note.

. Madam Mary Sa Itoiist all. who bequeathed 1,000 in 1730 for educating young men "of bright parts and good diligence for service of the Christian Church " Thomas Hancock, who founded the professorship of Hebrew and other oriental languages in 1764 with a gift of 1,000; John Alford, whose executors, acting in accordance with his wish that his money should be used to aid "pious and charitable purposes," nave 1,300 to establish a professorship " of s particular science of public utility "," Nicholas Boylston, who bequeathed 1,500 for the support of a professor of rhetoric in nil': ami Dr. K. ekiei Hersey, whose gift ablished a professorship of anatomy and physic in 1772, are other pre revo lutlonary names which figure on the list of Harvard's greatesl benefactors, t the Collegiate School of Connecticut the names of Kiihu Vale and Ii-v.

Dr. George Berkeley, with gifts of 500 and 400, res lively; at the College of New Jersey the names of Tennenl and Davy, of England, with a gifl of over 2.000; at King's the name of Joseph Murray with a bequest of his library and his estate worth ii'. HHNl in 1762; and at William and Mary the names of ies Blair and Etoberl Boyle give us other instances of educational philanthropy on a liberal scale in tin' colonial dayfi 4. oil'is I i; om TOWNS, CHI tu m. s, LNB S0CTI ins.

in addition to tin-r gifts from private individuals there i frequent evidence of Bupporl coming from town-, churches, and societies, in 1764 the town of Boston collected 476 by subscription, which it gave to Harvard to repair the lot. nod by the destruction of Harvard Hall by inc. Nine other towns made-mailer contributions to the same end, while two years previouslj ti

OS had made contributions to the college. Wheeled, received funds from public collections taken iii several eastern towns between 1762 and 1765 which wei. it value to Ida struggling school, to be known as Dartmouth ti ir ird v. i i, Appeodli xi it. foi copj (11.- Instrument! lift

M Qnlm 11. i. ii. i. Vol i,. mi; t. i i from Mi iidiik in hi agon l. mil. tiler. in 111-Col on let app ippeodlze In '. i i. of Qulni ii lorj uf Harvard.

, Vol 11, i' it-.

College." In the cases of Princeton, Queen's, King's, and Brown the donations from churches were large and frequent.

The Society for the Propagation of the Gospel in Foreign Parts found the colleges appropriate agencies through which to operate in the Colonies. As early as 1714 reference is made to a gift of books to the Yale library; in 1747 the society made a large donation of books to Harvard, and KM) in money in 17CA. TJ From the same society King's received 500 sterling and in 1702 a library of 1,500 books. The society also assisted in getting a collection made in England which raised nearly 6,000 sterling for the college in 1762. 30 The Society for Propagating the Gospel in New England and parts adjacent gave to Harvard 1,101 volumes and 300 sterling to repair the loss of its library in 1704. The Edinburgh Society for Promoting Religious Knowledge presented Harvard with some books in 1766, and the Society for Propagating Christian Knowledge, in Scotland, gave 30 for the purchase of books in 1769.

5. GIFTS OF BOOKS, BUILDINGS, AND LAND.

It is noticeable in the early years that many gifts of books were made to the colleges. However strongly the titles of the books may suggest the religious and theological nature of higher education, in those days such gifts were of the greatest importance when both the bounds and the methods of knowledge lay almost wholly within books alone.

There is an occasional gift of a building, and frequent reference is made to gifts of land. During the colonial period Harvard received from towns and individuals over 2,000 acres; 31 Yale received over 1,000 acres, including 300 acres from the general assembly; M King's received 5 acres in the heart of New York City, and 34,000 acres more from the State which were lost to the college and the State as well at the close of the Revolution;" Dartmouth received 400 acres from proprietors of the town of Hanover; " the College of New Jersey received 210 acres from the town and people of Princeton; and a large portion of Queen's campus was the gift of a private citizen. Gifts of real estate were for many years of little productive value however; so the chief support had to be money or something that could be exchanged at any time.

ANALYSIS OF THE GIFTS TO FOUR OF THE COLONIAL COLLEGES.

To get at the full meaning of the philanthropy of this period, however, complete lists of all the gifts to Harvard, Yale, King's, and the College of New Jersey, four of the nine colonial colleges, have been made and appear in Tables 3, 4, 5, and 6.

Remembering that it is not the absolute amount of a gift, but rather what the gift will purchase, that measures its value, we may ask, first: What was 18 Chase: History of Dartmouth, p. 31.

29 The motive back of this may be seen in the following quotation, which throws some light on the denominational motives which impelled many gifts. Referring to the gift of books: "A good investment for the conformity of four graduates of the Presbyterian College at Yale, Connecticut, had been mainly effected (in 17212-23) by theological works sent to the college in 1714." "Two Hundred Years of the S. P. G., 1701-1900," p. 799.

30 Ibid., pp. 775, 798.

81 Barnard's Journal, Vol. IX, 159, gives a full list of gifts of real estate. 12 Ibid., Vol. X, 693, mentions the important gifts.

33 A History of Columbia Univ., 1754-1904, p. 35 ff.

34 Chase: History of Dartmouth, p. 174.

the size of the problem which philanthropy had undertaken and what did education

1. SIZE in THE COLONIAL COLLEGES.

The numbers of students attending these colleges can be judged by the number of their graduates. Harvard rarely If ever had over 100 students be-fore the year L700, and at no time In the colonial period did she have.,. r 350 or-hx students, while Vale and King's had fewer still. Pennsylvania graduated in all only 135 students before 177;, Brown 60, and Dartmouth 31.

The teaching staff was also Bmall. The president's administrative d were insignif-icant, his chief function being thai of Instructor. Before L720 Harvard's faculty consisted of a president and from 1 r. u 4 tutors. At 3 i ihc president was assisted by from 1 to 4 tutors rarely more than:;. before the yai- 1755. After I7i'i Harvard's faculty gradually increased to 9; Yale's to 8; and King's to 11. In the ease of King's a much larger percentage were from the start of professorial rank.

Thus, judged by the size of student body and faculty, the actual work done in the colonial colleges was small, and great sums of money were not needed.

2. THE COST OK A COLLEGE EDUCATION.

The cost of a. college education at Harvard in its early days is shown in an Old account book for the period lg4i)-50 to 1059, from which it appears that for those graduating from 1653 to 1659 the total expense ranged from 80 25s 11 d, to 01 lis. 8id., or from about Slw to about 200 for four years' residence in college.

An itemize"! account of a student, Thomas Graves, of the. Mass of 1656, bj quarters shows that he paid about 32s. for tuition. His first quarter's expei appear as follows: M

Pounds. S. D. Qr.

0 r. i Commones and aiznges S s

Tuition, 8 a; study, rente, and bed, i;. viand iind. il. 2 8 It 0 0

Power loode i wood 17 4 0

The other three quarters' expenses were similar to this in 17!7 tins cost, according to an accounl of Judge Daniel Appleton White, given In volumi 6 ni the Massachusetts HI torlcal Sodetj Proceedings page 272, would b been about or the four yea!

Students' bills were often paid In butter, rye. malt, ho-, lamb, eggs, etc At Princeton, Muclean tells us thai a student's entire ezpensea In 1T 1 u proclamalin money.

fairlj complete account of the tuition cosl at Yale, as set forth in Table 2, data for which were gathered from Dexter'a Innals, shows the tuition not to have been much differenl at the beginning from the above account (tuition I at Ho rva rd a ha If cent urj earlier.

From Mo m-r Proc L800 1862, Vol. V, p. 60.

THE COLONIAL PERIOD. Table 2. Cost of education at Yale College.

1 In country pay 120 equaled about 60 sterling or one-third. 2 57 6s. Sd.

At Dartmouth in 1773 tuition and board together were 20 a year. At William and Mary the tuition in 1724 was " 20s. entrance and 20s. a year for pupilage for each scholar." A woman offered to " undertake the keeping of the college table at the rate of 11 per annum for each scholar, with the other advantages allowed to Mr. Jackson." ss At Princeton tuition was 3 in 1754, 4 in 1761, 5 in 1773, and board in 1761 was 15 a year, according to Maclean.

Reference to the prices of a few well-known commodities will help one to appreciate the apparently small gifts which we are to examine. In 1641 com-mon labor was worth Is. 6d. per day, the next year corn was worth 2s. 6d. ami wheat and barley 4s. per bushel. In 1670 wheat was worth 5s., corn 3s.; the year following labor was worth from Is. 3d. to Is. 8d. In 1704 corn was worth 2s. and wheat 3s. 8d. In 1727 wheat was worth 6s. 6d. to 8s. In 1752 corn was worth 4s. and wheat 6s. In 1776 corn was 3s. and wheat 6s. 8d. w 3. SALARIES OF COLLEGE PROFESSORS.

One further item of interest in this connection is the salary of the teaching staff. This was the chief item of expenditure in every college and is a fair index to the value of any gift or to the value of the funds available for the use of the college at any time. As shown in Table 2, Yale's president received from 60 to 300, while the salary of a tutor was very much less. Maclean thinks that Princeton's president did not receive over 50 annually before 1754. In that year his salary was fixed at 150 proclamation, rising to-J00 proclama-

M " Proc. of Visitors of William and Mary College, 1716," in The Virginia Magazine of History and Biography, Vol. IV, p. 174.

tion in 757 and to 4imi in i t. '. only to be reduced again to E2S0 with the usual perquisites, and finally to imi in itct. in 1768 H rose again to 350 proclamation, or about fi'ix; sterling, in it.". l' Maclean Btates the salary of a tutor t have been J sterling ami 66 in 17 7. The three professors at Princeton in i7t',7 received: Divinity, 17.".; mathematics, 150; language and logic, 125. In 1654 the overseers of Harvard College offered Rev. Mr. Charles Channing the presidency of the college at a salary of Mhi per annum. 1 ' From Judge Sewell's diary the-alary in 1698 appears to bave been i'im). 9

At the close of the colonial period Harvard's president uns receiving., hi i, a professor about 200, and tin librarian 60. in October) lt ".;. a committee of the colonial assembly of Connecticut reported that Sale ought to have: 1. A president, at lf0 per annum. 2 A professor sf divinity, at 11-". 6s. 8d. per annum.". A senior tutor, at ti. r Is. 4d. per milium. 4. Three junior tutors, at 51 Is. Id. per annum each.

Salaries at William and. Mary were little different. President Blair, the tir-1 president, received 150 at first, and later only 100, Increasing in 1755 t" iiix. During the same period a professor received 80 and fees of 20s. per student. In 17' ". each professor received 150, but no fees. In I77n the president received l'ihi. each of two divinity professors 200, two other professors each 1m. master of grammar Bchool 150, first usher 7.". second usher 40."

When one considers that the entire expenditures of Harvard for the year 1777 were but tins.; L8s. 2d. and that the college bad but 386 18a 2d. to pay it with, the residue being paid "by assessments on the scholars for study rent.

tuition, and other necessary charges, amounting oommunibus onnit i" about 7ihi; u or that lb." average annual Income Of William and. Mary College during the decade 1754 to L764 was 61,936 lis. r. jd." these salaries appear relatively high.

lilt. M II N OF PHILANTHROPE in Mil COLLEGES.

What now is the character of the educational philanthropy which was practiced in the midst of these conditions'." Was it Constructive,. r did it follow tradition? it might be bard to answer these questions to our entln tlon, hot an examination "(the parts of Tables " I 5, and o. which refer this p.-riod. will throw light on the BUbject.

iiih-j: Vol. I. App. n. lix I V - it.1.1 Vol. I, Appendli XI. p 190. " l i. i. t. v. t. II. p. I'll. ' Tyler, pp 187, H i quoted these. 1111 11r11 from the collage barear a booki Williamsburg, it. Old Colonic Capitol, p, I

"gun. II. p, 241

"ii. i. Lyon;. " Williamsburg, the Old Colonial Capital," p. I

Table 3.

-Donations and grants to Harvard University, 1636-1910 Distribution of the donations by individuals?

Those before L851 were taken from Qoincy's 1 These data were compiled from three sources mainly. History of Harvard I'ni Harvard College" publi:

Those for the years 1852-1910 were taken from the annual reports of t he president College.

Gift of 27 acres of land, Income to be used for scholarships for students from town of Dorchester.

Data for the years 1862-63 and 1867-68 are not included.

1 University, 2 vols., published in 1S40, and from thelists of 'Grants and Donations i published in Barnard's American Journal of Education, Vol. IX, pp. 139-160,8ept., i860.; 1852-1910 were taken from the annual reports of the president and treasurer of Harvard

Tabu i. Donations and grants to Yale University, ?" 1900 Distribution o donations by individuals

L710. 1711-1715. 1716 1720.

1721-1725. 1726-1730.

i:: si 1736 1746 1750.

17." I 17. V.

1761 170.". 1770 1771 1776 1780.

17-1 17. 'I 1795. 1800.

imii L805.

1808-1810.

l-il 1815.

1820.

i! donation: iy individuals given to colony.

11,335 3,627 2,679

Total donal by individuals.

i:!4 1. W0 1,282 1,424 .".., 116 1,971 1,041 103 62 1,290 3,233 1,458 1,122 IIMI

HKI IIMI l-il 1845 1846 7-. sis 14,664 12,000 l 14,648 l 17,000 i-'7 95 ible: Conn. Col Records; Doxtoi i i m bull ii. im.

Vol. II; 1 H! Book; h ddw In n i (arm w in. h ih ortb i io, oo l i i pei yew New Haven HI Vol. I, p. 1 J0.

Tasle f. Donations and plants to Princeton University, Vt S-1856 and 1006-1010 Distribution of the donations by individuals. 1 1 Data for this table were taken from Maclean's Hist, of the College of New Jersey; Murray's Hist, of Educ. in New Jersey; and from reports of the president and treasurer of the college.

2 In 1860 the library contained about 12,000 volumes, practica'ly all of which had been donated. See Maclean, Hist, of thecollege of New Jersey, Vol. I, p. 206.

3 Right to conduct lottery.

There were three sources of income for the colleges: The general court, philanthropy, and student fees. In the accompanying tables we are concerned with that of philanthropy mainly, though for comparative purposes, column 1 gives the amounts received from the State.

The gifts are grouped into five-year periods. Column 2 gives us a picture of tlitstream of donations that has been flowing for so many years into the treasuries of four of our oldest colleges.

The first large grouping of the gifts is that which shows them to have been given to the college unconditionally on the one hand, or with certain conditions which wholly or in part determine how the money shall be spent on the other. The next grouping is that which states whether the gift is for present use or for permament endowment. Further than this it is a question of just what is the specific condition. Is it for the library, for scholarships, for apparatus, etc.?

FUNCTION OF THE STATE IN HIGHER EDUCATION.

During the eighteenth century Harvard received relatively much more from the State than in the seventeenth century. Yet during the entire colonial period the loss of that support would have been almost fatal to the college. The same

Tabus 6.- Donations and grants to Columbia University, r)-i9i0 Distributions of the donations! individuals. 1 ' Tin-.1 it f. ir this tnliii were taken from ai official publication of the university entitli 1 'i fim 11 he treasurer of ttic u 1904 Tin OOVei ilic (Olumliii i uri'iiration lone mid does not incliulf true of: c and Columbia. For Princeton, however, there Is; i different ry. Only once during the colonial period was any: ii l given bj the State to Princeton, in 1762 the assembly granted the righl i" hold: i lotterj for au amount not i ' "-i 5,000." This was verj real help, and Bince n Involved; special. hi ui the legislature it Is ralr i" assume thai it biiowb friendliness mi the pari "i the State. few years after iiiis period rinses, the State granted the coll nnnuallj fur three years, i" ' paid In quarter!) paymenl in the report f the rommittee which represented the college before the leg lature ii appears thai legislators ra sed the objection thai the Institution w under the "sole and exclusive control of one denomination of Christians." Tin. difficulties with which this ad was pn sed nnd tin- resull of the ad show the extenl to which the College of Men Jersej wa nol; i State Institution.

irtean, Vol I, p 13, ni. i cop) of the report. f committee appointed lo appl; i"
ii. sun. fni aid.

It is said on good authority, declares. Maclean, that not one of the legislators who voted for the act was returned to his office at the ensuing election, so bitter was the feeling against the act."

It is to be remembered that New Jersey, unlike Connecticut and Massachusetts, was settled by people of several different religious sects, and that while religious education of the Congregational type practically meant State education for Yale and Harvard, it meant only church education for the New. Jersey college. 48

A more careful study of the problem of higher education and the State is inviting, but a few illustrations to show that State education of collegiate grade. while understood and practiced in part, was not a fully established educational social philosophy in the colonial days, serves our purpose. Wheelock's Indian school received aid, 50 per annum for five years, once from the Colony of New Hampshire, and after the school became Dartmouth College it received aid of 60 in 1771 and 500 in 1773. after which no formal request was ever made, though one was prepared in 1775. 49 New Hampshire apparently had no thought of Dartmouth as a State institution.

The College of Rhode Island was essentially a denominational school established in a State where the Baptist faith predominated but by the church of that denomination in several Colonies. There should theoretically have been no hindrance to making their college quite as much an object of State concern as was the case with Yale, Harvard, and Kings; but the facts show that little help was ever received by the college from the Colony, due, no doubt, to Rhode Island's insistence upon a real separation of church and state.

At William and Mary the relation of college and state varied with the governors of the province, several of whom were exceedingly unfriendly to higher education in general, and to President Blair and his college in particular. But in spite of these the college received much genuine assistance from the Colony. At the outset it was granted a duty on liquors imported, and on skins and furs exported, which by October, 1695. amounted to 441 sterling."" and "upwards of 3,000 pounds com mini thus annis." 1 In 171S a grant of 1,000 was made by the Colony to establish three scholarships (part of this fund was invested in negro slaves). In 1726 a grant of 200 annually for 21 years was made from the duty on liquors. In 1734 this increased to include the entire income of the 1 penny per gallon duty on liquors, providing that part of the money should be used for the purchase of books, each of which was to bear a label, reading " The gift of the General Assembly of Virginia in the Year 1734."' M In 1759 the college received another grant in the form of a tax on peddlers. Without making the list exhaustive, it is evident that the State took an interest in the college and bore a fairly substantial part of its financial burdens, even if it did not assume the real responsibility.

CONDITIONAL AND UNCONDITIONAL GIFTS.

In the case of Harvard there seems to have been a gradual and fairly persistent tendency for people to specify how the college should use their gifts. At Yale there was somewhat of a general tendency toward unconditional gifts, 7 Maclean, Vol. I, p. 18.

During and following the Revolution Yale could not get help from the State for much the same reason. The legislature demanded that " civilians " be placed on the board of trustees before the State rendered aid. This was finally done.

Chase, pp. 272, 277.

60 Bruce, Philip Alexander: Institutional History of Virginia in the Seventeenth Ten tury. Vol. I, p. 395.

S1 Howe's History of the Colony of Virginia, p. 325.

18 This is another evidence that the State did not consider the college a State institution.

but most of the early gifts were conditional. At Princeton also there was a tendency to place ondition upon the gifts, and with the emphasis in the early years somewhat between that for Vale, which emphasizes conditional and thai for Harvard which emphasizes unconditional gifts In tin' early days a college was just one thing, li was a teaching Institution (lily ami there was little occasion for giving other than "to the coll Vet many gifts were carefully safeguarded with conditions.

glance at the succeeding columns of the tables, nowever, ami an explanation ot ' the large figures in the "purpose specified" column will su t show that the main current, even of the conditional iritis, was generally in line with the fundamental aim ami practical needs of the college. Taking 7.". per cent in the "purpose specified" column ot the Harvard table, I planation i 60 vorth of books and 251 15s. 6d. toward "the repairs of the i 99.5 per cent in 1671 1675 is largely accounted for by the contributions from II towns "for the erection of a new building for the college," amounting to over 2,000. The 90 per cenl In 1696 1700 Is mostly accounted for by the cosl of Stoughton Hall, buill and presented to the collt by the Hon. William Stoughton in 1699. The first ion percent In the "pur it'nd " column of the Princeton table was gifts to the aid of pious and indigent students, a very common mode of assistance in those days, as ii is now in many colleges. In the Vale table the firsl 100 per cenl refers to bo for the library, and the second to nearly 1,000 volumes, mostly from England.

i. ll PRE8EN1 i si FOB ENDOWMENT.

uext general grouping of the funds is Lato these for present use ami these for permanent endowment, it is very noticeable that ail through this period the gifts were in the main t" he used at "ni e by the college. The "dead hand," good or bad. plays in i In this period of our educational history.

The 1"" per cent In the Harvard table, "permanent endowment" column, 1646 1650, was just one bequest, and that to the college In general. Th 64 per cent in 1666 1670 was for ti 9tablishment of "two fellows and two

The T." per cent in ltb". 1730 was for the maintenance of preachers and for the education of pieus young men for the ministry, both entirely appropriate to thi of Harvard at that time. This Bame tendencs appears to hi n t rue for 11 t her colle mow Gil is u i;; i CONDITIOrs

What ami how nian, kinds of tions were placed upon the-, III the there a.-d gift8, fll fit ill number, and thin the main object of the college, but gradually In nun d variety until In the present da3 i i elj num. reus.

During the period under on, however, thej were few In n ber. They for buildings, for the library, for aid oi plou for , nil f lo for equlpmi nl. and for p I di nonAj oirrs i pon nu qbow mi oi uj. i . hat to broaden tin purpose and fund Ion of th I n car be i ited numerou It an ni'w field "t work has been undertaken bj n rol th r mil of such o entll oc ad botanical gard un Illustrations of this, in the colonial days, however, when tin' economic: inl social life was restricted; when for the raosl part professional Life meant the ministry, arid a ministry whose profession rested upon accepted truths and philosophies long ago written down in 1 ks, and nol upon abilitj ami training in the discovery of new truth and the making of new creeds; when all learning was book learning; we expect the conditions placed upon bene factions to reflect these ideas and conditions.

To say that "endowment" has not produced an educational experiment until it has completely departed from the common aims and ideas of people in general, however, is to restrict the meaning of educational experiment. The founding of a professorship of divinity in 1721 was an experiment in a way. even though theology was then the center of the college curriculum. If this professorship did nothing startling by way of educational experimentation, it at least slutted the emphasis in the Harvard curriculum, which means that it made Harvard a slightly different Harvard from what it had been.

So. while an examination of the tables shows that nothing very unusual was started by gifts during this period, it also shows that without the gifts the colleges would have been different from what they were.

A study of the gifts "to pious and indigent students" is especially interest ing. Yale seems to have received nothing for this purpose before 1825. The same is not true, however, for either Harvard or Princeton. The fact that the tendency to add to these funds to-day, and that they are of such large consequence in our theological colleges particularly, gives us a special interest in the early ancestry of this particular kind of beneficence. We can not help noting the absence of such funds in our modern scientific schools. To say that our present research fellowship is the same thing is not true. Competitive scholarships and fellowships are very old methods of helping students and not in any way connected with the funds here considered. In colonial times the condition almost always read " for the benefit of pious and indigent students of the gospel ministry," br words to that effect. Since a large percentage of colonial college students were training for the ministry, 53 it is perhaps unfair to assume that indigence was regarded as a virtue or proper qualification for entering that profession. The income of a minister was about equal to that of a professor, so the economic outlook for the theological student could scarcelj be responsible for the ministry calling its members largely from the indigent class. Whatever the explanation, it seems a fact that colonial Harvard and Princeton did subsidize a class of students who classified as " indigent, pious, and desirous of entering the ministry."

The plan of establishing scholarships and fellowships, granted on basis of scholar-ships and general ability, appears first at Harvard in 1643, with a gift of 100 from Lady Moulson, of England. There were very few such funds established in the colonial period, but there were enough to show that the idea, old in Europe of course, had been brought into the colonial college.

The. uifts for the establishment of professorships, usually regarded as on the whole the most useful of all conditional benefactions to higher education, 51 have played some part in the development of our colleges since the first ift for that purpose in 1721. when the Hollis professorship of divinity was established at Harvard. From then on these gifts take a prominent place among Harvard's benefactions, and there are a few such gifts to Yale and Princeton. Table 7 will show, in order of their establishment, the kinds of professorships which were established in this period, the field of work each covered, and how each was endowed.

"See " Professional Distribution of College and University Graduates," by Bailey B. Burritt, U. S. Bii. of Educ. Bui., 1912. No. 19.

M See President Eliot's Ad. Rep. of Harvard Univ., 1901-2, p. 61.

l i; i. k 7. Distribution uitd character of pre-Revolutionary professorships.

nity

Gift by Thos. Hollis. Harvard. W an- nuallv. B rd lift by Tho i

"philosophy.

nit y Gift by Philip Ln ind other oriental : if' Prii eton.

be richolasboylston Barvard l, n00 sterling.

, nig.

erling.

Here are six professorships three of which are divinity and two others more or less allied to divinity, four founded bj bequest and two bj gift, all iut one "ii a fair foundation and that one soon enlarged by subscription founded in the half century preceding the Revolution, which, when considered in the light of the small faculties of thai time, represent a very substantial accomplishment for philanthropy. The fields covered by these professorships were all entirely legitimate, in fact essential to the meaning of h college that time. We must not overlook the fact, however, thai such a gift was not made at Harvard during almost its first century of work, at Vale during its tirst half century, and at Princeton for 20 years. The preeedenl for fount professorships K of course, very old In Europe, and it is a t it surprising that such endowments wen- begun so late In the Colonies

The endowment of the library is scarcely second in importance to thai r professorshi- The column representing gifts t" the library is only partially complete, since so man: of the gifts wore in books and manuscripts, the value nt" which was only occasionally t" be found. The monej gifts t libraries during this riod, including f i ks when value was Btated, were more prominent in Y ile than in Harvard or Princeton.

The form of the gift varies somewhal with the college, but In all the li percentage of bent a for this period are b3 dirt Instead of bj be- quest. Thl for li rvard, more so for Princeton, and pronouncedly for Vale. The bequt often presented for permanent rather than for Immt though Ihej have no! bt itetl here to show i. i riod should be taken ol the Important , i(iii pro for the Infant e for i 1 iiown for Harvard only Prom enl thai tht had ma nda in the mother i uintry. In fact, without tin what

Harvard avenues of t he i hurcn and mot h e are often e ld r-oni were fi

When n ar hi n I he f ' 11 i '- pport, valu than one, rapldlj dried ! nut tl period la h and Influent e In out higher education. So it is, and the ending of the column of figures here referred to is a concrete statement of one of the things thai is meant by the ending ol the English influence.

When we consider those figures in the light of the developments which the gifts opened up and Hie suggestions they brought to our colleges, we have more than a word picture of this transition stage in one of our higher institutions of learning.

There is one table (Table 6) not yet referred to, dealing with King's College, later Columbia University. The fact that this college received so little by way of donations through this period, and a fairly regular amount from the Colony, makes it a marked exception. This study is dealing with philanthropy, and not with the lack of it, and can only pass this with the suggestion thai the political life of New York, the religious restrictions attaching to the foundation of the college, and the general and growing attitude of unfriendliness which the people felt toward the English church, and also the English Government, made it more difficult for the people to sympathize with the college and treat it as an institution of the people. Without attempting to analyze the cause further, it must he referred to here as a marked exception to the ride of college building in colonial America: and in view of the fact that gifts for other colleges not infrequently came from people in New York, we can only inter that the people themselves were not neglectful of higher education, hut only of this college.

SUMMARY AND CONCLUSIONS.

This concludes a description Of the educational philanthropy of the colonial period. If we were to try to characterize it briefly, we should say that, in the light of the economic conditions under which a group of young colonies were forming, it was extensive and that it was consciously focused upon a vital social problem. We should say that organized religion dominated practically all the colleges and a large proportion of the gifts, and often denominationalism tried to bend the college in this or that direction, most often with little iil effect. We should say that there is good evidence thai a very large percentage of the gifts were solicited, usually for a specific purpose, and that therefore the conditions of many gifts were actually determined by the college authorities themselves, which argues that, after all. the colleges did not take form to a very marked extent in terms of the ideas, or v ' 'ms either, of philanthropists. We should say that the restricted gifts which. cut to the colleges were focused in reasonable proportion upon the fundamental needs of the schools, such, for instance, as buildings and grounds (not shown separately in the tables), professorships, library, ami scholarships. We should say that the unrestricted gifts, though in relative amount they varied for the three colleges, show a substantial and fairly dependable source of support for each, and that the tendency to give for immediate needs was as commendable as it was pronounced, when we realize the limited resources of the colleges.

We should say also that there is evidence in the foundation documents and facts pertaining to the actual establishing of the colleges thai they were all William and Mary a partial exception intended from the star! to rest upon philanthropy, and that the important service of philanthropy was not in its money and property gifts alone, but in responsibility borne and service rendered, service which meant not only self-sacrifice to a cause but constructive thinking and planning.

Wlble the colonial governments rendered most important service to William and Mary. Yale. Harvard, and King's, though not to Prii ton. Brown, Dartmouth, and Rutgers, it dues not appear that in any case the Colony frankly ni fully accepted th responsibility for developing a college. State aid to i."i- education was an accepted facl when we think of Massachu Con oecticut, Virginia, and New fork, bul not el ewhei i in these cases there explanations made which do nol fullj justify oui calling anj i them si. institutions in ill" present accepted sense. If there is in this a lesson for modern philanthropy, it is in the pe h which the gifts flowed iiit the colleges under all circumstances, and the I sane directions under which th ts did their work.

Chapter III. THE EARLY NATIONAL PERIOD, 1776-1865.

THE PERIOD CHARACTERIZED.

The treatment of the years 1770 to 1865 as one period iu the history of educational philanthropy is a more or less arbitrary division of time in the nature, extent, or methods of giving during these years. Vet there are some reasons, aside from cenvenience, tor studying these first 90 years of our mi tional existence as a single period.

As was pointed out above, the gilts from England practically ceased at the time of the Revolution. The Colonies now became independent States, and began to face grave social and political responsibilities. Not only were the ties with the mother country broken, but new, and for future educational development, significant friendships were formed in Europe with peoples whose educational ideas and institutions were quite unlike those of England. In losing this important source of support and influence, in forming new political and, as it proved, educational ties in Europe, and in facing her new political future, all American institutions enter upon a new period and must learn to function in new terms.

Once a Nation was established, its next great, political crisis was in 1861. During these years there had been remarkable political and industrial achievements, important religious movements, an unheard-of expansion of population to the west, and numerous and varied social philosophies had been tried out and proved failures in practice.

All these movements and ideas were mere or less reflected in the development of higher education. There had been a decline in interest in education, succeeded by an educational revival; there had been a rapid growth in the number of colleges; the Nation and the States had shown an interest in education by the ordinances of 1785 and 17S7 and by the actual founding of sev-eral State colleges. It is mainly to philanthropy, however, that we must look as the chief agency in the development of the American college during these first 90 years of our national life. To trace the development of colleges through these years, and to describe the part which philanthropy played, is the problem of this chapter.

THE NUMBER OF COLLEGES AND HOW STARTED.

So far as mere numbers of institutions are concerned, private giving bore the larger part of the responsibility for higher learning during Ha' early years. The States took no very definite step before 1791. and then in most eases followed rather tardily the lead of private and church-endowed colleges. What the States did, however, was not Insignificant From the foundation of Uar. ri down thej had contributed liberally to higher education. 1

While making nn occasional grant upon request from a college is different from tak ng full responsibility, yel we must remember tw n things: F stairs were themselves in process of making and had do traditions or pr dents t follow in such matters; second, private and church-endowed education had centuries of precedent and traditions to point 111 way, In other words, society had been accustomed to using the church and private agencies t'iii- handling its college problems, and it is uot surprising that it was Blo in placing that function upon the State.

During this period, then, one maj saj that the Ideas of State support and control of higher education worked themselves ut. but that the chief burden rested upon private and church donations.

This is brought out-till more clearlj in Table 8, which shows the names of all ilio Siatrs added to the original '-' during this period, the dates of their admission, the name, date, and source of control of the first college estal lished in each, the date when the State college or university was fonnded, and the number of colleges which had been founded in each State before the state university was established.

There are '." Stales in this-roup, and in only 2, Nevada and Florida, was the State university the first institution of higher education founded. In three Others, however, the State and a privately endowed BChool were stalled iii the same year, a comparison of the date column-, in the table will show that in most cases the State was more than 10 years old before it established a State college or university. This was doubtless due in most cases to the fact that the state was already well supplied with colleges; as appears from the nexl to the last column in the table. One other set of fact in this table is of inter. viz. the control of these colleges. Ill nearly every c; ise it Was the church which did the pioneering. Those marked uonsectarian were usually none the l religious project-, and some of iheui so marked were originally denominational. Philanthropy, for the most pari through the church, i- therefore not onlj re sponsible from the standpoint of of colleges throughout this period, but also for the actual college pioneering of the ever broadening frontier of tin. new country.

Williams College (1793) received ' ' for 1 building for free icl I L798, 1,200; in 1816, three-six teen t ha of tbi M i f. i i" equaling (130,000; in 18.19 a moli I ' Back in is., to Colbj Collei e (181 t of M; i sachu ed Btati i folio? from Mai acbusetta in L813 a township of land, and again In 1813 a township (land; from i. i for 7.- 11,000 annuallj for I I to In i Indlgi 1861,! balf town adltlon thin colli I,000 bj Apt i 1863 In t etoulld (ater nn (1821), In 1827, In IS i In 18 and in nti d Bowdoln I llvs.

of land; In I l, f pi anuall) "until the leglslalun shall . in i v annually I eginnl i

Table 8.- Date of establishment and sources of support and control of the first college or university in each of the States admitted before 1865.

THE BEGINNINGS.

During the Revolution higher education received a brief setback, but soon showed a tendency to keep pace with the growth of the population. The story of the beginnings of practically all the colleges founded during this period is one of penury. They were not launched with large foundation gifts or grants, such as were common at the close of the century, but most often by small gifts collected by subscription, as the following illustrations plainly show:

Williams College, founded in 171)3. grew out of a free school established in 1755 by a bequest from Col. Ephraim Williams. 2

Bowdoin College, founded in 1794, received its first important gifl of 1,000 and 1.000 acres of land, worth 2 shillings an acre, from Mr. Bowdoin.

. Middlebury College, founded in 1S(X), started with 4,000, made up of small donations from the citizens of the town of Middlebury.

Amherst College, founded in 1821, began as an academy started by a subscription in 1812 and as a college with a subscription of 52, 24 t, known as the charity fund.

Oberlin College, founded in 1833 as one of the manual-labor projects, started with a gift of 500 acres of land, worth about 1.50 per acre, supplemented by the usual subscription plan.

Mount Ilolyoke Seminary and College, founded in ES."Hi, started on small sub-scriptions, 1, S00 of which amounted to 27,000.

Marietta College, founded in 1835, received her first funds of: s., iioii by SUb scriptions and erected her second building on funds raised l subscriptions at 2 per subscriber.

'This bequest could not have been large, fn- iu I7sn. upon request, the State granted its trustees; i right to raise 1,200 by lottery, the proceeds to be used lu erect a building for the free school.

A very large number of-n as academies. The idea i . rown i i ma to bavi been.-in accepted prirj(L in pbilant ropi nd srate edncalion alike."

Of tii' 1 i i colh inded between the close of the Revolution and tin- open ing of tin- nineteenth century, Williams, Hampden-Sidney, Union, Hamilton, Washington and Jefferson, and Washington ami Lee, all began as academies or schools of that rank, with practically n funds. The Btorj of this period is therefore a storj of simple pioneering, ami that on a small scale.

now fill. WORE WAS ACCOMPLISHED.

Prom tho above it is clear that higher education was to he largely supported ami directed by the church. The college was a definite pari of the plan to propagate the Christian religion, ami early in the new centurj the cry for an educated ministry was voiced by almosl every religious publication. Response to this need in the form of church hoards of education will he discussed later.

it must he pointed oul here, however, that between the years 1830 ami 1850 the number of theological seminaries increased from- to 38 This religious work in founding colleges is often denominational, as may be -con from the fifth column in Table S. The older colleges in the Easl sent missionaries into the new countrj across the mountains to meet the " spiritual i dies of the western country," as an officer of one of the earn, declares. Table '. shows that all bul 33 of the colleges of this period were established by philanthropy, i '7 of the UT1 being distinctly denominational proje. t and 71 others being religious hut nonsectarian.

Tabij '. Vumber of colleges, universities, and technical schools established during the thri number under tin various types of control.

Thus the work of philanthropy through this period is to remain where it was in colonial lime in the hands of the church. hen, DOthin illy new by wi ieral motive or machinery for putting that motive to work.

Religion trii- to meel it- problems bj training for religious ami political leadership, it does this in ihe band-to-mouth fashion to which it has ion.- been umed. Williams, Amherst, Mlddlebury, Hamilton, and Oberltn were ' ' oul. fii VIII, 1782, "" t for founi eh. former kirlitliitiirea (tale s i" their foundi bo aundrj la. we foi the 'ii, hi of ' of Latin, Oi o i wril and H"' like, Inten " oi ii nine I'. v i.-t !. in tii. ea11" a lai hut in etui phy, useful and ornamental aru and

Qu V, p. 331, founded wry much as were Harvard, STale, and Princeton. The problems they hoped to olve were much the same, and the methods of carrying on their work were practically the same, with the exception that early in the new century the churches began to develop boards of education through which a now type of philanthropy, aimed directly at the preparation of a trained ministry, was administered.

Further detailed study of the development of philanthropy in the older foundations, in typical foundations of this period, and of church hoards of education should bring to light any new ideas or methods of work which the philanthropy "f this period has to offer.

PHILANTHROPY IN THE OLDER COLLEGES. 1. A PERIOD OF SMALL GIFTS, SMALL INCOME, AND. SMALL ENDOWMENT.

To follow out the developments which took place in the older foundations we have to refer again to Tables 2, 3, 4. 5, and 6, where the data discussed in chapter 3 are carried forward.

These colleges passed through the stormy period of the Revolution, in which they all suffered more or less. Yet they survived, and an examination of the total columns in these tables seems to indicate that the spirit of philanthropy was kept alive through it all. The total gifts to Harvard during the years 1771-1775 were relatively large, though they dropped during the decade following. Yale and Princeton, on the other hand, received but little by way of gifts during this period, but came well up to their average dining the decade following, while King's College appears not to have been affected seriously.

Aside from a few large gifts just before the Civil War. this was a period of small gifts for these old colleges. Harvard depended upon small subscriptions to erect Divinity Hall in 1S26, to establish a professorship of natural history in 1S05, and a professorship of geology in 1S20. More than three-fourths of Yale's endowment fund of 100,000 was raised in 1831 and 1832 by Wyllis Warner in a similar way. 6 It was also a time when permanent endowments were small, and when the colleges were often struggling with heavy deficits. Yale's income from invested funds in 1831 amounted to but 2,300, while the income from tuition was too small to cover the necessary expenditures of 15,474." In appealing to the legislature for aid in 1822, Yale declared her debt to be 11,000, with permanent productive funds of but 20,000. In 1S25 Harvard's expenditures exceeded her income by more than 4,0U0, while as late as 1840 her productive funds amounted to only about 156,126." Rhode Island College changed her name to Brown University in 1804 for a gift of 5,000.

An examination of the total columns in these four tables shows that it was not only a period of small gifts but also one of small total income. With the funds that were at the disposal of Yale in 1800, it is not surprising that the ambition of the college to become a university could be satisfied with the establishment of schools of law, medicine, and theology in terms of a single professorship for each of those fields.

G Baldwin, reissue of "Annals of Yale," appendix, presents list of subscribers.

"Steiner, B. C. Hist, of Educ. in Conn., p. 152, Washington.). ('., L893.

7 Quincy, "History of Harvard College," II, 360, makes the former or those statements on authority of the treasurer's report of that year. The second is from the treasurer'! report of 1840, ibid., appendix No. LX.

KPANSION Ol THE COLLEGE INI) INCBEAS1 01 CONDITIONAl GIFT8.

Our concern here is not with the re size of the gift, however, but par ularlj with the i litions upon which the gifl ia received. Is.1 colli expands from one to many buildings, from; i classical to ntific program, from one to many instructors in other won!-, from a traditional college to a university its needs tend to become more and more diverse, and so, specific, is opposed t" general. The donor who in the old daj saw only the colli now sees laboratories, various kinds of professorships, buildings, libra) departments of this and that, etc., and it' not consulted about his gift, la less likely in give to the "college," since the college has now hen. me a vague and indefinite thing.

Amid such developments we should expecl gifts t" be made less frequently id the general minis of the institution, and more often to a single specified part of it. An examination of columns four and five of our tallies show- that this was roughly the tendency in all eases. The per cent given to "general fund," with some exceptions, gradually grows smaller and the per cent to " specified purposes " la rger.

The question arises as to whether the new departures were more often Initiated iy the president or board of trustee or bj sum,, donor who conceived idea and proposed its adoption by offering to endow it. 'This ran not be answered fully for the reason thai all the facts concerning the naming of con ditions upon which a gifl is offered can nol now be obtained. It appears that must uf the gifts of this period were conditional. While it is true that the new professorships, by way id which new departments and schools were usually opened up, are named in memory of some special donor," yet we can not be a that growth In these terms was not largely directed bj the colli 3. How 1 HE GIFTS w 1 ia. 1 ON Dl I toNED.

second question of Interest about a gift is whether it is to be available For Immediate use or p become a pan of the productive funds id the colle During colonial times, as was pointed out ubove, gifts were most genera 11 j for immediate use. Thai is slightly less true for this period, as may be s,. en from a studj of columns six and seven of the table, h Is decidedlj less true for Harvard, whose " permanent endowment" funds show i, growth all through the period.

further tudj of these tables will show the conditions nnder which the y narmw stn beneficence flowing Into I. dually widened during these DO years. The librarj column would be enlarged if all of the uld have been Included, it appear– ti1.1t the librarj ed proportional! Pale through this period than II had Peon re 1 no monej gifts went to the llbrarii umbiu and at Princeton, while al Flarvn I Increased slightly and became more constant.

Tl 1 professorship ever founded in this countrj was thai Initj at flnrvard, endowed bj Thomas Flollls in 1721. There were Ave others founded in Harvard, Pule, and

Prlueeton during the colonial 1 1; 1. after which onstanl I Harvard and Princeton are for tin- puri i

Pale no gi) purpose are recorded froi Vfter tl date however, then a fnlrlj regular and 'Mai tendency to endow Instruc lion Columbia ha had much lesi of tin kind there having been .- gift 'in 1848) pre. He year 1896 1 he de velopments in this particular Line of giving coincide roughly with the period of expansion of the little traditional college into a university.

Reference to the "pious and indigent students'" column in these tables shows that at Harvard the girts to this cause are irregular and relatively less than in the earlier years: at Princeton they become 1 v regular and relatively larger. At Vale, where jao such gifts appear before 1821, the response is irregular and slight. At Columbia practically no gifts are for the " poor and pious."

Assistance to students direct conies through another channel (see scholar.-hili and fellowship columns of the tables), in which poverty and piety play no part. It has long been the custom to give money to pay the tuition of the brightest student, as judged by competitive examination, and from our tables this continues to be supported. Before 1835 Harvard and Princeton show much more interest in the poor and pious than in this group. Yale tends to favor the competitive scholarship idea, and at Columbia, where the poor and pious receive little or no attention, a large and constant proportion of gifts go to scholarships and fellowships.

One other way of helping the student directly is by use of prizes. Account was kept of such gifts, but they proved to be irregular in all cases and of no great consequence, so they do not appear in the tables. By adding together the two items "scholarships" and "pious and indigent students" in the tables we see that there is much educational philanthrophy which chooses to go directly to the student rather than indirectly through provision of instructors, library, laboratory, buildings, etc. It is not the large educational enterprise in which such donors are interested; it is an individual, and philanthropy is with them a personal matter, that is, true charity.

4. LARGE GIFTS OF THE PERIOD.

There were a few large, gifts received during this period. Leaving out the funds raised by subscription, the important gifts to three of the old colonial colleges during this period are recorded in Table 10, which shows their form, date, amount, and purpose.

Table 10. Amounts and conditions of the large gifts to Harvard. Yale, and Col a in bin from 1776 to 1865.

It would certainly be difficult to question the conditions placed upon thesp gifts. There are 13 in all, 5 for the founding of professorships, 4 for buildings, 1 for endowment of a scientific school, 1 for scholarships, 1 "on specified con ditions " which tire not known, and 1 unrestricted.

e gifts represent departures but nol wide departures from the ordinary college. The French influence is seen in the establishment of a French and Spanish pri ship, the flrsl of its kind in this country. The influence of the scientific movement also is shown by the professorships of natural historj and mineralogy and geology which were established in i s ' and 1820.

Ir is noteworthy that but one of these gifts is to go to the student direct. The conditions of the gift provide that young men of rare powers in any department of knowledge be helped, not only after they enter Harvard but even before, wherever they may be found.

Tims it appears that the large gifts of this period provided only for normal expansion of the colleges, and probably did nt anticipate, excepl In point of rime, the growth that would have come had these colleges been provided with unconditional instead of conditional gifts.

Reference to the dates will show how few were the gifts of this size previous to the middle of the nineteenth century. As t form, those to Harvard and Columbia are mostly by. while those to Sale are bj gift direct 5. FORM OF TIIK GUI S.

Turning again to the last two columns of 1 for a study of the form of the benefactions, we find that at Harvard there Is a slight lucre in the "bequests" column during this period, but thai at Vale. Princeton, and Columbia the burden f the income is by direct gift.

in these tallies, then, which are doubtless typical for all the older colleges, the developments show that the total gifts to the colleges do nol increase much before the second quarter of the new century. By that time income from the state had grown very irregular or stopped entirely. There wi encj to change from giving "to the college" to giving to some special feature of the college. Permanent endowment received more attention than before and there was a falling off of interest in the " pious ami Indigent," except at Princeton. There was an increased interest in scholarships ami fellowships and a rapidly growing interest In prol: and gifts rather than he quests, Harvard excepted, remained (he favorite form of heiiefact ions. I II! l v I HROPT IN Mil. EGE8 FOUNDED LAT1 R, n already, the increase in the number kept pace with the develo untry, the church continu or the motion of higher education. A large percentage of the collegt definitely lominatlonal p aimed at the development ol a trained ministrj and the of re and classical I among laymen. Thej were often the i ih of academies, man of which were Btarted on verj small tin ption (as Middlebun I o ege from an acadetnj with fill:' ' 0

Bi ol ii Ider coli veloped lai people of. the Easl who had moved w promoted bj the blch had fo ed the olonia s, M i lean i. i ' to ii,. ' tbi u i The following Ognrm Hh' t i amount of undor very similar frontier and financial conditions we expect the collegi as well as the nature and methods of their support and control, I" resemble those of the older colleges in the East. In general, in Cacl one could almost say in detail, this resemblance did exist.

Amherst College is typical for the period. In Table 11 is shown a distribution of its gifts from its origin in 1821 to 1890. The college originated Amherst Academy, a subscription fund for wh ch was started in 1S12. The school opened in 1S14 and by 181S was beginning the collection of funds for the future college. Amherst is one of the nine New England colleges founded during this period and began its career both as an academy and as a colli on money collected by subscription. Its first funds,. 51,404, were collected to found a "Charity Institution." and the great care with which the conditions controlling the administration of this fund are set forth" impresses one with the missionary zeal of the founders. Article three of this document provides that live-sixths of the interest of the fund shall be forever appropriated to the classical education in the institution of indigent pious young men for the ministry, and the other sixth shall be added to the principal for its perpetual increase, while the principal shall be secured intact and perpetually augmenting. 11 Here, in the conditions controlling this foundation gift, is evidence of the religious aim of the college and of its acceptance of the policy of subsidizing young men who qualify as "indigent, pious, and desirous of entering the ministry." While not the same in detail, this sounds much like the beginning of a colonial college.

For a number of years Amherst's history has much to say about poverty, but a comparison of the total benefactions to Amherst in her early years with those for Harvard. Princeton, and Yale in Tables 3. 4. and 5 shows that Amherst fared somewhat better in her infancy than did these older colleges, even allowing for differences in money values. In the face of her fairly real competition for funds with Harvard. Yale, and 'Williams, on the average her income compares favorably with that of Princeton during the years 1821-1830, and then rapidly surpasses Princeton, Harvard, and Yale for a number of years.

these gifts by years from 1S44 to 18S4. This is mostly the work of the Congregational Church. If the many other church societies did as well, then this represents an important source of support for western colleges.

1844 15, 5.88 1845 9, 500 1846 14,000 1847 12, 555 1848 10,000 1849 34, 300 1850 41,500 1851 20. 500 1852 10.000 1853 13,496 1854 11.

1855 L5, 1856 18, 1857 12, 1858 8, 1859 10, 1860 18, 1861-62. 10, 1863 14, 1864 56.

These amounts were contributed to the following institutions:

Western Reserve College, Ohio. Marietta College, Ohio. Lane Theological Seminary, Ohio. Wittenberg College, Ohio. Heidelberg College, Ohio. Oberlin College. Ohio. Wilberforce University. Ohio. Illinois College. Illinois. Knox College, Illinois. Wabash College, Indiana. Beloit College, Wisconsin. Ripon College, Wisconsin. Washburn College, Kansas.

Iowa College, Iowa.

Yellow Springs Co wa.

German Evangelical College, Missouri.

Webster College. Missouri.

Thayer College. Missouri.

Drury College. Missouri.

Pacific University, Oregon.

College of St. Paul, Minnesota.

Carleton College, Minnesota,

College of California. California.

Pacific Theological Seminary, California.

Olivet College, Michigan.

Berea College, Kentucky.

11 See W. S. Tyler, "A History of Amherst College," p. 7 ff. Cor a full statement of the 14 articles controlling the fund.

13 The report of the treasurer of Amherst College for 1912 shows this fund to be 95,098.50.

PHILANTHROPY JN AMERICAN Hli. HI. K EDUCATION.

Table 11. Donations and grants to Imherst College, 1821 i of gifts t; i individuals. 1

Distribution im which thi i. i W. S. Tyler, "A History of Amherst College Qe ' ary Bush, Hist, of High) Known as the charity fund. I. of income to he added to principal annually. In hi ollege treasurer shows this fund to le 95,098.50.

To show bow completely acceptable this new college was to the people, however narrow and local its constituency, we need only to 1 k at the attendance and size of the teaching staff from the beginning l '."i. While thi e was; i serious drop in attendance about 1840 to 1850, there steady I

Tlic tuition charges for these years were as follows: 182 i-:::: 30 (33 27 7 33 1836 1M7 1855 1864 L868 15

L868 1871 75 i-, i 1-7:.;

L875 l; 100 1886. n Ii i– evident thai the Income from tuition was nol great, and Blnce In the earlier years of the college nothing was received from the State, practically the ivhole burden was carried by philanthropy. Blow this was done is of Borne interest.

Table 1 a fair description, one striking feature of which is the final column, which shows vvhal per cenl r all ifts were obtained bj the sui- ription method. Aside from this the table offers little that is differeni from what we have seen in the older colleges for this period. Mosl of ii"- gifts have! ondltional, but when we i u at the follow amns In the table that pro iii is. library, and buildings 11:1 fared bo well, it appears thai the conditions placed upon the Kifj v weri ns of real neede In the earlj years, as in the older colleges, mosl "t the gifts liable for Imn ise, with a Blight tendency toward permanent endow de from the charitj subscription at the beginning, which Is a Bcholar- p fiimi for ministerial students, ti" scholarships were founded fill 1857, when about P50 wt 11-tn- 1 Bat little m 13 for prises was received dur- . that Hi amount of gifts direct to studen s, aside fn foundat mall in comparison with that given to tin- llbi. nr for bulldini

Profi il t. ell bj thej ni la the older colleges during the Used after th tl gift As at Yale, Princeton, and Columbia, mosl of the benefactions arc by gift rather tban by bequest.

THEOLOGICAL EDUCATION OF THIS PERIOD.

Tn 1011! 13 there were 179 theological schools reporting to the United States Commissioner of Education, 70 of which were founded during this period. These schools show permanent endowment funds of nearly 40,000,000, and since they are all the work of philanthropy and have from the start constituted a prominent feature of higher education in this country some consideration of the methods of philanthropy in their development is pertinent to this study.

The first separately organized school of this type founded in the United States was the Andover Theological Seminary, established in ISO'S. Tin-lengthy creed of this school was carefully prepared by the two wings of Calvinists and has been publicly read and subscribed to by each professor on his inauguration and hefore the trustees every fifth year since the foundation. 13 This is how strictly denominational the school has been.

In 1913 the school reported a plant worth 300,000 and nearly three-quarters of a million dollars in permanent endowment funds." It received initial gifts of buildings and 60,000, and before the close of this period possessed five endowed professorships.

Table 12. Gifts to permanent funds of Andover Theological Seminary, 1H01 to 1890. 1

Dates.

1807-1810 1811-1815 1816-1820 1831-1835 1841-184.". 1856-1860 1866-1870 1871-187.". 1876-1880 1881-188.". 1886-1890

Total amount.

75,000 79,000 25,000 15,000 80,000 53,000 119,000 95,000 240,000 14,000 315,000

General fund.

30,000 80,000

Professorships.

45,000 79,000 25,000 15,000 25,000 43,000 50,000

Library.

25,000 20,000 '2s,"666'

Scholarships.

97,00!) 1 Data for this table obtained from Geo. Gary Bush's Hist, of Higher Ed. in Mass., 1891. Of this amount, 10,000 was for the establishment of a lectureship.

Table 12 shows the distribution of the permanent funds of the institution. From this table it will be seen that no great part of its gifts for permanent endowment have gone to the general fund, that nothing has gone to scholarships or to indigent and pious students or to prizes, but that many gifts have gone to endow professorships. Only 28,000 of these amounts seems to have been received by way of small subscriptions.

The Bangor Theological Seminary was established in 1814 by the Society for Promoting Theological Education. This was one of the earliest education societies in America. Its purpose was raising a fund to assist those well-disposed young men that are desirous of entering in the work of the gospel ministry, but by deficiency of pecuniary resources are unah e to prosecute a course of regular stud es necessary to qualify them for a station so important and useful." "The Maine Charily School," as it was then called, was established for the purpose of promoting religion, morality, etc. Only native-horn citizens could ever become trust

Bush, p. 240.

14 Rep. U. S. Com. of Edu., 1013, p. 325.

16 Hall: Higher Educ. in Maine, p. 35.

In the early days the school had no endowment and marks its first important gift as 300. in L835 a 100,000 endowment fund arted, bul because of the financial crisis of that time only about one-third of this amount was sed. Another effort was made in 1849, when 34,000 was raised Cor the dowmenl of two professorships, since that date the school has prospered. In 1913 a permanent endowmenl of 310,000 was reported.

These are but samples to Bhow how philanthropy, entirely unaided by the State, took care of education for this particular profession.

OTHJ R LINES OF PROFESSION 1. TRA1 NINO.

'h: it philanthrophy has not done is f some intere I here, since we an-concerned with its relation to the development of all higher education.

Fheology has been kept strictly apart from politics in this country, and ic from a few early gifts frpm the State, this profession has been built up entirely by philanthrophy. lis institutional growth was in the beginning in (. Million with colleges of liberal training, hut toward the ch. se. r the eighteenth centurj began in develo parate schools. This wis partly in tcai' of Hi'- rather unorthodox trend in the colleges ami partly in order to better the instruction, since the demand for a better-trained ministry appears in have been strong. D nominationalism was also a factor in the case of churches which had imi established colleges of their own.

While higher education for the ministry has been handled entirely by philanthropy, this has uot been true of either law or medicine, a few professorships of law "; and physic were established in the universities before the end of the colonial period, but appear to have been t, academic ami indii ti the rather utilitarian motives of these two professions in the beginning, in fad all through this period, and even later, a few busy doctors taught medicine, and law was learned almost wholly by apprenticeship plte the rapidly increasing Importance of the legal profession after the Revolution. 1 I Li CATION OF WOM I NT.

Another Important educational movement In the history of higher edu which tes during this period, and furnishes new motives to phll thn that of collegi women. The movement takes Its rise along with Jncksonlan democracy, nntlslavery agitation, the great westv ve 11 it-it t, and early women's rights agitation, and very quickly takes permanent form in the hands of philanthropy, first through the pioneer work ol Mrs. i i11:1 Wlllurd m the founding of the Troy Female Si m 1820 ami later work-if. Mi.– Mary Lyon in connection with th founding "i Mount I p.; i! ollege in '

And- an in" educational career, Mrs. Wlllard opened the Troy in 1821. An Initial fund ol d bj the tj and promptly supple nted bj gift Vi ordlng! the curriculum offi It la fair i" look upon tb pnulne ami ml attempt."t higher education for women, even though th bc! i latei pai out "f exlsten in ever e this was a philanthropic entei ii succeeded as such for some rt which tunc It wielded a very wide Influence and

Wlllli. li, t'nl ai Columbia In 1 1801: at 1 fertmonui in nd:. i Elnrvbrd In 181 - i mid i ii B Bar- rltt. 18 f Ed. Rep., 1 i. pp. 240 21 I stood as one of the important foundation stones which Mrs. Wlllard laid for the higher education of women in this country.

Miss Lyon, like Mrs. Willard, proceeded on the assumption that it was quite as important to enlist the interest and sympathy of the great mass of people as it was to secure funds. She planned, therefore, to raise 30,000 by small subscriptions to start Mount Holyoke Seminary and College. When one reads that one of the record books of subscriptions contained the names of more than 1, S00 subscribers from 90 places, promising a total of 27,000, in sums varying from 6 cents to 1,000," and then reads that it was Miss Lyon's wish to " put within the reach of students of moderate means such opportunities that none can find better a permanent institution consecrated to the work of training young women to the greatest usefulness."' and one " designed to be furnished with every advantage that the state of education in this country will allow,

20 he realizes that, while philanthropy is not finding new methods, it is finding a new motive in an institution exclusively for the higher education of women.

As is well known, the new idea met with opposition but, as usual, it wis finally proved that philanthropy can be depended upon to meet any important social need as soon as that need differentiates itself from mere vague unrest.

This movement for the education of women was less than 30 years old when the founder of Vassar College laid down funds amounting to nearly 800."io for a similar institution, so much in demand as to attract nearly 350 students in its first year. Thus in a short time philanthropy's experiment had succeeded far beyond expectations.

PHILANTHROPY AND THE MANUAL-LABOR COLLEGES.

The manual labor movement in American secondary and higher education came to this country from Europe, where for nearly the first half of the nine teenth century Fellenherg and his successors experimented with the idea of combining remunerative work with school training. Students from mam countries visited the Fellenherg institution, and the movement spread rapidly, the labor features finding a fertile field in both colleges and secondary schools in this country- In Connecticut as early as 1819 such a school was established, and in 1831 the manual labor society for promoting manual labor in literary institutions was organized. The secretary of this society made an extended tour of the West and Southwest, visiting the manual labor schools, but seems to have left no statistical evidence of his study.

Where the idea was introduced here the labor feature was used as an appeal to the philanthropist for support and to the parent to send his son to college, whore, as a Wesle. van University resolution of August 27, 183.;. says, "the physical as well as the intellectual and moral education will he attended to."

It is only necessary to state that this idea took form in Maine Wesleyan Seminary in 1825, in Andover Theological Seminary in 18' 'G, in Colin College in 1S2T. in Western Reserve University in 1830, in Wesleyan University in 1833, in Hartford Theological Seminary in 1834, and in Oberlin from its origin in 1833, to show something of the type of colleges which introduced it and the extent of its adoption. It was an expression of a new social as well as educa 10 Mount Holyoke Seminary and College, by Mrs. Sarah D. (Locke) Stowe, U. S. B-. i. of Ed. CIrc. No. 6, 1891, Ch. XXII.

"Mofmt Holyoke College- the Seventy-fifth Anniversary," i. 13.

tional philosophy, and seei is to have made it appeal for benefactions from the social, moral, religious, educational, and economic points f view.

a more intimate study of the benefactions t" Oberlin, a college founded after the movement had become popular and one which fairly hewed Its way Into the world mi the manual-labor basis, should give as a fair picture (this typ of educational philanthropy.

Mr. Leonard, 9 quoting from Oberlin's Ural annual report, 1834, says: "The manual labor department is indispensable to complete education" and, "in a word, ii meets the wants of a man as a compound being and prevents common and amazing waste of money, time, health, and Life." Be then r "s on to explain the nature ami extent of the department and how well ii Is working, in 1837 nearly all the young ladies and a majority of the young gentlemen have paid their hoard by manual labor." This report adds thai while the school's funds wen- as they found them at thai time, no pledge could be made that labor would be furnished, from then on the failure of the scheme was oiil a matter of time, and in L849 the trustees realized that it was ool paying and thai some legal means of ending the experiment musl be found.

Ii was at this point that the "dead hand" appeared. The 500 acres of land had been donated to a manual labor school. In ls. Legal authority was found for leasing the ground, the lessee covenanting "yearly, during said term, to employ students of said college in some department of manual labor (when applied for) and pay them tor their labor the current market price, to an amount ouch year of, ii least- J for each acre of hind hereby demised." 18 Further on in the lease it is agreed that in;,-,. any part of the lease is ad judged t be beyond the powers of the Oberlin trustees, the lease becomes void. Tin- expression "manual labor" disappeared from the catalogue after 1867 68, and ii place of it reference Is made to "facilities for self-support."

Thus within ' ' v; ns from the beginning the college had failed to met the full demand for Labor, ami within 20 years the labor Bcheme had disappeared in failure. During those 20 years, however, Oberlin had become a fairly well-iblished college, though these had been years of extreme poverty with much debt.

The Bchoops first real funds, some si:. mmi. were received during the Bret elj upon solicitation in payment tor scholarships. 11 The busini side of the undertaking soon used this m y. and the college went begging io,. York, where it received a guarantee for full endowment of eight pro Ipi n unalterable condition of this gift, which was never paid, was that N(houkl i" given equal privilege with white students in the school.

in i i we have an Illustration of how the policy of a. oil. r. q t Ing a very Important social and political issue wns to be absolutel settled bj philanthropy, and settled contrarj t the wishes of oearij half the trust of the college Becond effeel ot this intended gift was the abolition of all tuition cha move which cost the college dearlj ithln 10,000 in debt tn 1887 an effort i endowment realised onlj about 6,000 ' Finally, In 181 i Ibvihi I. I i' ird, p 221 ft ulflon, m ii-iy i: i Ing the ii lil. s wny.

feature would I perpetua agents were scut t England to make an appeal for help with which to pay tin-debts of the college. 2 This brought 30,000 and valuable collections of books, and deserves notice here because the agents carried with them to England letters from antislavery leaders in America through which they presented their ease to antislavery sympathizers in England. This and the idea of educa tion for women are said to have made special appeal to the Society of Friend-in England. 39

Little aside from a gift of 20.000 acres of land was received during the next decade, but in 1850 an attempt at endowment was made, and by 1852 almost 95,000 was raised and invested. This, however, was another sale of scholarships, which this time secured free tuition for one student perpetually for 100, 18 years for 50, and ti years for 25. This was merely paying tuition in advance, but a little figuring will show that it must be counted an absurdly low tuition. The interest on 100 could not possibly pay the cost of educating a student. Thus the college increased its business, 27 but on an unsound economic basis, which broke down with the high cost of living in the sixties.

This is a fair picture of the relation of philanthropy to the manual labor college movement. There is little to distinguish it from the philanthropy in the old colleges where the manual labor idea was never adopted. It is just more evidence that philanthropy in education has been governed by the conditions of the times rather than by any wise educational philosophy. The manual labor college was but an incident in our great westward expansion.

Such cure-all schemes in education were essential to the times. Hartford Theological Seminary carefully avoided the "incubus" of any permanent fund for the first few years, but when her subscribers fell off and lost their zeal for giving, an 11,000 bequest was gladly accepted as permanent endowment.

Kenyon College sent out an appeal, "The Star in the West, or Kenyon College in the Year of Our Lord 1828," calling upon the reader to send 1 to the struggling school. " Kenyon College Circles " were formed in numerous town3 where women met and sewed for the college, and more than 25,000 was sent in as ti-? result of this appeal

On the whole it is wiser to say that the manual labor movement was useful because it expressed an essential element in the civilization of that time than to say that it was useless because it was educationally and economically impossible.

PHILANTHEOPHY THROUGH EDUCATION SOCIETIES.

Another channel through which philanthropy has played a part in American higher education is that of religions education societies. These societies began to organize early in the nineteenth century in response to the demand for trained missionaries and ministers. Statistics published in early numbers of the American Quarterly Register show that churches were fully conscious of this need.

Aside from several small local societies, the American Education Society" was the initial undertaking in this field, its original constitution being dated August 20 Fairchild: Oberlin, the Colony and the College, p. 208. Ibid., p. 209.

27 This immediately increased the number of students from 570 to 1,020.

28 In 1874 the American Education Society and the Society for the Promotion of Col legiate and Theological Education in the West were united under the name American College and Education Society. See their annual reports for 1874.

29, L81J The aim of this soeietj is made clear by the Following Btatemeot from its original conslitution:

Taking into Berious consideration the deplorable condition of the inbab tants nt' aited States, the greater pan. i whom are either de i com petenl religious instruction or exposed to the errors and enthusiasm of un- ned men, we,,, hereby, form oui Into a society for the benevolent purpose of aiding, and aid, Indigent young men of talents and hopeful piety in acquiring a learned and competent education for the Gospel. Ministry.

This outlines a definite piece of work i be done, proposes philanthropy ae means, and indigent young men of talents and hopeful of pii ty us the agency for doing it.

Further "ii in the constitution it is proposed to raise funds b cription, and it is stated thai " a i ermanenl fund, of which five-sixths pari of the inten-t only may be expended, shall be formed of bequests, leg.-i-. donations, grants, and subscriptions," and further, thai agents shall be appointed t" solicit by exciting churches and congregations to make annual collections for this purpose; and by establishing auxiliary societies in towns, counties, and distant regions, together with Cenl Societies, by personal and persevering addresses to rich individuals of both sexes. and by respectful applications to legislative I nd other i Is C men; by establishing active and extensive correspondences, etc.

All appropriations of funds are to be made by the trustees, who will also ei selecl the candi lates for the charity. All i nts of the charity who do net cuter the ministry musl refund the inonej 1. The tinal article declares that "This Constitution, but ool Its object, maj be altered and aim nded."

The plans by which aid was granted have been changed from time to time, ' i hi i Bince I s i- the money has in en given as a gratuity.

The bases for eligibility of applicants for assistance are staled in general terms only. Up in mi the applicant musl have had i; months of classical studies. During 1843 this was Increased to 12 months, and in 1842 to colli entrance requirements, with the exception of third-year academy students in some casee This exception was Later abolished.

Such ha- been the general aim and plans of work of one of tin oldest of these etles in America. To describe the workings of the other societies of this type would be practicallj to repeal the above The Presbyterian Education lety was founded In 1819, became a branch of the American Education So eiet. in 1827 ' and operated as such until the break In the Presbyter an Church, which took place toward the close of the period under The bo tor educating pious young men for the mlnistn of the Protestanl Episcopal Church wi d in ims and within a decade bad 28 auxiliary soclel

"A eopj of ii i const it ii i tun If printed In full in tppendii of the uinaaj re-

Whetber tbl f organising edui for the training (minister! wai borrowed frum Etogland i wh known, tnit uch.,.

i, i- iii- aiii'-i lean Quarterly Register, vo " pp uik-model for thi of itadenl I abilities a(tbe university, and prin iiv in order to tbe ministry," fallowed b wbicb were . oui "i t. i in iv. if tbe Hi "iii we read i "Tbal tbe schouu t, bopefol f r godll :. hi pari. of 'hi Ingenious Mi position, and nol a miiii ii Oxford: i n i! an bridge nt i b i. it.-j. f. i " o Barnard's i tar J.-f Bduc, rol it.::;:: ff. " An. Bep

THE EARLY NATIONAL PKIilon, 1176-1865.

operating under its supervision." The Massachusetts Baptist Education Society, later tire board of education of the Northern Baptist Church, starting in 1814; the board of education of the Reformed Dutch Church, starting in 1828; the board of education of the Methodist Episcopal Church, starting in 1864; and tin-Society for the Promotion of Collegiate and Theological Education in the Wesl are the principal organizations of this type. Each of these had numerous branch societies, and all supported students in part or in full by loans.

The development of branch or auxiliary societies in connection with the American Education Society is a fair sample of their methods. Between 1815 and 1838 there were organized 63 branch societies east of the Mississippi River and north of the southern boundary of Tennessee; 41 of these were founded between 1829 and 1834. 3

Although the chief method of work was by direct gift or loan to the student, in some cases professorships were established, salaries were paid, and buildings erected. The gifts or loans to students were often no more than 40 per year.

In 1829 to 1831 there were IS to 22 theological seminaries in operation in the United States. Table 13 shows the number of students attending these schools and the number receiving aid from some education society. 34

From this it appears that from one-fourth to one-sixth of the theological students in the United States at this time were beneficiaries of these organizations.

Table 15 sets forth for each fifth year, which may be taken as representative of the other years, the financial history of three of these societies, along with the numbers of beneficiaries they have had under their care during this period.

Table 14 shows what a large part of the student body at Amherst College was veceiving assistance from the American Education Society.

Table 13. Number of students in theological seminaries and number receiving aid from religious education societies.

Table 14. Number of students attending Amherst College. 18 '(5-185. and number and per cent of these receiving aid from the American Educational Society. 0 o Data for this table taken from Edward H. Hitchcock's Reminiscences of Amherst College.

"Amer. Quar. Register, Jan., 1829, p. 190.

"From An. Rep. Am. Educ. Soc. for 1S39, pp. 88-90.

w Data taken from Am. Quar. Register, vl. 1, p. 220; vol. 2, p. 247; vol. 3, p. 303.

PHILANTHROPY IN AMEBIC AN RTGHEti EDUCATION.

Tabu 15. Showing far each fifth year the annual receipt and thr number of students aiih ti by three church or religious educational societies.

! Compiled from the volume oi ih. n Quarterly R ual reports of the

One of these societies, the Society for the Promotion of Collegiate and Theological Education in the West, bad a slightly differenl purpose. It was organized in 1844, and operated as a separate society down to 1874, at which time it joined with the American Education Society. Its purpose as sel forth in its charter" was to assisl struggling young colleges in the Wee with funds collected In eastern churches." It was concerned with general as well a- with theological training, and limited Its aid uot only to western colleges but only to Mich of these as showed promise. There Is evidence thai this societj bad influence In the development of higher standards In western colleges."

Table ig. Financial account (the Society for the Promotion f Collegiate and Theological Education in the West, mowing the work done by the Boclety, will bear close Btndy. The c aid "to the College," QOl t" individual Students, and did this In a ;. down undertakings and to stimulate useful ones n we compare the Income of th ties with that of colleges reported in

Tables '-'. 8, I, 5, i". LI, and L2, we win-. thai in these earl years the work,, i the lea is bj no means a mere Incident In tin- educational machinery.

annual r.-i. i i. i s 11 m,,.(. affecta iin- ii.-. i-h. hs of the i lifth hi, re 1848,; anuaj n poi i foi 18 IS, p t'-'.

From 1821 to 1825 Yale received by gift approximately 16,000 annually; Princeton loss than 2,000; Harvard about 12,000; and Amherst less than 4,000; while the American Education Society received close to 14,000, the Presbyterian Society over 5,000, and the Baptist Society some 1,500.

We have pointed out that the ministry is the only calling for which training lias thus far been subsidized in this way. The law, medicine, business, and technical pursuits have made their way by force of their economic importance to society. Has it been true that religion represents a " real " but not a " felt " need or has it been ti ue. as Adam Smith would argue, that such procedure will overstock the occupation in question?

The actual demand for ministers is shown in a convincing maimer by statistics published in the American Quarterly Register and in the annual reports of the societies. 38 That the demand was large is- obvious from the fact that of all the graduates of 37 of the most prominent American colleges, from 20.8 per cent to 30.8 per cent entered the ministry in every five-year period between 1776 and 1S65. 39 Important as this profession was, the demand did not bring forth the supply, even with this special care. In this connection we must not overlook the fact that entrance to the ministry was by much longer educational route than was entrance to either the law or medicine, and without citing facts we know that it was not more remunerative than these other fields.

It follows then that something had to be done to meet the situation, and these education societies were the response which the churches made. With all the obvious waste the method involved, it not only did much toward the support of an important profession but it also supervised and helped to popularize the demand for higher education.

SUMMARY AND CONCLUSIONS.

In summarizing the development of this period we may note that the English influence practically disappeared with the Revolution and that State and National support continued.

Before the end of the period the idea of a State college had taken definite form, though the real burden still rested upon philanthropy. In nearly every State the church and private enterprise did the college pioneering.

Small gifts and the subscription method were as common as was the poverty which characterized the financial history of practically all the colleges of the period. Few, even of the older colleges, found themselves well endowed by 1861.

It was a period in which the old traditional college curriculum and organization yielded to the influence of the developments in science and to the broadening business and professional demands. Consequently, it was a time in which the conditions attaching to gifts were more numerous and perhaps more varied than in the past. In spite of this, there was a growing tendency to develop permanent funds.

These tendencies are as characteristic of the new as of the old foundations, and in both the conditional gifts tend to go mainly to professorships, library, and buildings; that is, to the institution rather than to the student direct. While there is some increase in interest in direct assistance for students, it is given, Princeton excepted, on the basis of scholarly promise rather than on that of indigence and piety.

88 See an address of the board of education of the Presbyterian Church (their first annual report, 1819), p. 14; also their annual report for 1843, p. 5; and tbe same for 1867, p. 5.

Burrltt, p. 144.

The early financial historj of the newer colleges of the period is Identically like the beginning years of the old colonial group of colleges, ut they grew much more rapidly.

During this per od als we bave tl e b nnin of several new ideas In higher eduu tion, which open uj i ral aevi lines of philanthropic activity the i velopinenl (' professional schools, b education Bociel and i he manual labor college.

in the development of schools of medicine, law, an are Btruck bj the fad that, from the standpoint of their scientific development, medicine and law achieved but little during this period and that very Largely on the b of private venture institutions, while tl logy was taken over by philanthropy and became well established, first as a department of the older co and later as separate schools. In the development of the thi cal schools de- non.11 naturally played an important part, and the lering of funds by the separate denominations from their own churches was the common pracl

Colleges for women offered; i new motive for giving to education but noth ng at all im'.". by way of a method of directing the use to which gifts should be put.

When the law of supplj and demand railed t provide enough ministers, philanthropy came at once to its rescue with education societies which played a large part in higher education during the period.

manual labor college was the most unique though not the most valuable venture in higher education undertaken during the period, it Called, but I was an experiment that was fully warranted if we consider the times In which it was tried, and surely ii is balanced bj the success of women's coll)

Whatever the value of the various experiments, it was philanthropy that Initiated and carried them through, as it was mainly philanthropj that red the new country and philanthropj that kepi the old colleges alive through these rs.

Chapter IV. THE LATE NATIONAL PERIOD, 1865 TO 1918.

THE PERIOD CHARACTERIZED.

The period from 1865 to 1918 is quite unlike the colonial and early uational periods in several ways. The rapid increase in population which began before the Civil War has continued, but has brought a foreign class far more difficult of assimilation than was that of pre-war days. With the rapid development of machinery have come remarkable industrial and commercial expansion and remarkable means of communication and travel. The free public land has fast disappeared, bringing with it a demand for new and technical methods in agri-' culture. The corporate method has been widely adopted, and large private fortunes have been amassed.

Along with these changes have come many new things in education. The idea of State support of higher education has been fully established; more than a dozen large private fortunes have given rise to as many institutions of higher learning; and some 8 or 10 large nonteachiug foundations have been established. During this period a new interpretation of education has been developed in accordance with the findings of the newer sciences of sociology, psychology, and biology, and given concrete expression in the organization and methods of our institutions of higher education in the botanical garden, the laboratory method in all the sciences, in the- free use of the elective system of studies, and in the broadened college entrance requirements.

GROWTH IN NUMBER OF COLLEGES.

Just how philanthropy has adjusted itself to these new conditions will now be shown. First of all, the relative number of colleges founded by philanthropy is a rough index of the extent, if not of the character, of its work.

At the beginning of this period the tendency to found private or church institutions was at its height, since which time the number has gradually decreased, till now very few are being established by either State or philanthropy, not so much because there are universities enough as because the changed meaning of education and the new conception of a university have ruled out the type of enterprise that tended to subsist on enthusiasm rather than on funds.

The new demands of this period have no more balked philanthropy than they have the State. If, however, consideration were given to the number of institutions that ceased to exist, it would be seen that philanthropy had very often overstepped its mark.

Soon after the Civil War, due very largely to the national land grant act of 1862, the movement for State schools began to assert itself. 1 Now all States have their higher institutions of learning, largely endowed by the National Government, but resting firmly upon a State tax.

1 See Kandel, I. L. Federal Aid for Vocational Education. The Carnegie Foundation for the Advancement of Teaching, Bui. 10, 1917.

Table 17. Date 0 esta ent and source of support and control 0 tin college or university in h of the States admitted subsequently t t8

Nebi. ka.

rado

North Dakota South Dakota.

. bington.

Wvomiii 1 tkluhoina.

Mexico.

Arizona

Admitted first institution.

Name.

State I Qiv ' 1 ni ersil r

Jame ma College of Agriculture state University

Agricultural College

University of Arizona !7 1 1881 1850 1891 1891 rol.

te univi hoof ab- h-hed.

Istl 1-77

Number of ool 1 lished before State

Since 1865, T ' new States have been admitted to the Union. From Table IT we are able to see thai for the most part it was the State rather than philanthropy thai did the pioneering in higher education in these States. In; of the L2 stairs higher education was well under way before the State was admitted to the Union, in 8 of the 1- stales the first such school. ibllshed bj the state, while in the remaining 1 the church lead the way, and In n-i little had been done before the stale Institution was rounded.

This contrasts rather Bharply with the facts brought out in Table '. which shows these same facts for the early national period. Here v. dealing with Western States, for the mosl part verj sparsely Bettled, whereas Tabli refer- to Eastern and Central States, somewhat more densely populated. The hlef explanation, however, would Beem to be not that the missionary zeal of the churches, philanthropists, and educators was lagging, but rather that the idea Of Slate higher education was getting under headway and that the national grant of 1862 came at an early date in the development of the West 1 ne number f church and private foundations since established ahows that the efforts of philanthropy have nol Magged. Should the State, or private and philanthropic enterprise, determine the meter and amount of higher education? And related to this, what powi should be granted i private or church endowed Institutions? The Btruf between these social theories, a notable early date In which is that of the Dartmouth Collegi Ion In 1819, does aol begin In L865, it began In 1 . iih the opposition In Nevi Jersey Colony and elsewhere to sectarian control of the college which the colonial government wa 1 to help support ii began In a real sense m Revolutionarj daya and In the daya when Amerl . democracy orna as a nation, hi that time It; is urged tl since higher education will d much toward determining national ideals, the

Stale should direct and control it; and lh. opposite, that the Sta-hi I t to be taxed to lead anyone's son to college. 11 Is Interesting that Presidents

White, of Cornell, lot, "I Harvard, hit p f Ihis issue at the beginning oi thl period

Probablj it Is corn that this dash baa provided the; Btimu in-, to growth ami expansion that has been fell i higher education through Id. I imly CSLB do little more than call. mention here to thl Interesting theoretical developmei

THE LATE NATIONAL PKRIOD, 18rj5-l!)18.

GENERAL SURVEY OF EDUCATIONAL PHILANTHROPY. IN THIS PE-RIOD.

Practically from its beginning in 186S the United States Bureau of Education has included in its annual report statistics bearing upon the work of philanthropy in education. The following tables offer a fairly competent general picture of the extent and character of philanthropy in higher education since 1 71. From Table 18 it is possible to see, at intervals of five years: First, the annual contribution to higher education from city. State, and Nation; second, the amounts contributed by students through tuition and other fees: third, the amounts contributed by productive funds held by the colleges; fourth, the contributions from philanthropy; fifth, the contributions from all other sources; and. finally, the total annual income of all institutions of higher education. Resides these is stated the wealth of the United States in billions of dollars, and the population by millions for each decade.

The steady increase in income from each of these sources as the years pass shows not only the rapid growth of higher education but the dependability of each of these sources of support. When the total column, or any single column, is compared with the growth in national wealth, it is plain that higher education is more liberally supported each succeeding decade. It will be noted that the "benefactions" column does not show the degree of increase that is shown by the first column or by the " total " column. This, however, is to be expected with the rise of the State colleges in this period. But it will be seen that benefactions are not quite keeping pace with the rate of growth in wealth, (hi the other hand, the rate of increase in wealth is surpassed by the growth in income from productive funds, most of which funds have been established by philanthropy.

In comparison with the growth in population, it is obvious that each decade is providing more educational facilities of a high order per unit of population than was provided by the" next preceding decade. We have here to remind ourselves though that the per capita wealth has shown a far greater rate of increase than is shown by any of the other figures, which suggests that educational and philanthropic enthusiasms are not outrunning their purses.

Table 18. Sources and amounts of income for higher education in the I nited States, each fifth year from 1871 to 1915

Compiled from the annual reports of the U. S. Commissioner of Education.) 1 From 1S71 this table includes universities and colleges for men and for both sexes: after 1905 techiun logical schools are added; and after 1910 women's colleges are added. Before 1888column 1 Include from State only; in 1S90 it includes income from State and city; and after 1891 it includes income from States, cities, and United States. Column 2 includes only tuition' down to 189S, after which it include "other fees" (board and room rent). The figures in any given line, thai is. for a rygiven year, are fully comparable. In comparing the figures for one year or period with those of a later year or period, the above facts must be kept in mind.

"For year 1 904.

8 Estimated.

For year 1870.

Table 10. covering the period From 1 71 to 1885, including gifts to secondary as well as higher schools, shows tha on an average more than half of all gifts hi i" "permanent endowment and general purpos What part of this w.-is available for immediate use it is not possible to determine; nor i-it possible to say what were the special conditions placed upon the gifts.

Table 19. Total benefactions to all forma of education and ii" per cent of that total given under the restrictions indicated.

Prom a study of the "professorships" and the "fellowships, scholarships, and prizes" columns, which are not included in the "endowments and general purposes" column, it would be natural to Infer that much ot column two won I to general unrestricted endowments, from the standpoint of growth in i manent endowment funds, however, the whole table, as a single sample of evidence, is quite reassuring. Furthermore, there is little to criticize In evidence available on the nature of the conditions placed upon thi

A fairly considerable amount has always been given unconditionally in the past, if we Judge bj Individual ea which have been cited in the last two chapters, and here is evl hat this was true in general over the i through these 15 years. The "to indigent Btudents" column Beems to Indicate that what was true in the ea tudied wus also true In- 'neral.

In Table 20 la shown, from the tribution ol three I- 1907 to 1915, Here there is no mlal the f i'h nee I over thi an ln i Interest in giving i" iii ' permanent endowment o er education in this table the

"ciiiiic. Deludes ail "ai which onlj the h i be c bining the tl ile 19 which represent gift. s to i Tii i.-il 1 ' nt endowi al pneral purp In column one endowment, which til see a clear Indication I ot fund- now than was t rue od. 11.-i' to " plant and equlpiw I ike a bet it-how . i than in Table L9 in both there is much fluctuation Hie c with thi ruble 19, Improvement In quuntlt;

A third collection of facts compiled from the United States Commissioner's reports and presented in the following tables furnishes evidence upon which we may generalize regarding the character and extent of benefactions to higher education through this period.

Table 20. Benefactions to higher education in the United States and the per cent of that total given for endowments, for plant and equipment, and for current expenses.
Dates.
1915 1914 1913 1912 1911 1910 1909 1908 1907
Total gifts.
310,124 670,017 651,958 783,090 963,145 755,663 807,122 820,955 953,339
Percent for-
Endow-ments.
Plant and equipment.
Current expenses.
Table 21 shows the number of schools of theology, law, medicine, dentistry, pharmacy, agriculture, and mechanic arts, and of women's colleges that were opened during each five-year period since the first one was founded in 1761-1765. No account is taken here of colleges that have failed.

Three forces have assisted in the development of these schools the State, philanthropy, and private enterprise. Philanthropy is almost, if not solely, responsible for the schools of theology. The State and private enterprise, with some help from philanthropy, have developed the law schools. All three are responsible for the medical schools, though private enterprise is playing a smaller and smaller part. Philanthropy has shown very little interest thus far in schools of dentistry and pharmacy, but has contributed liberally to colleges of agriculture and mechanical arts, which latter have been fostered mainly by the State. In most cases the State provides coeducational universities but not special schools for women. 2 The women's colleges Included in this table are therefore the work of philanthropy and private enterprise.

Table 22 shows the part that philanthropy has taken in the development of these colleges.

The table is not complete, but one can not run up those columns without being impressed with the strength of the appeal which these fields of higher education have so continuously made to the people. Gifts for the higher education of women have increased with fair regularity and to a creditable extent.

rilll. AN THUmpY IX AMERICAN Ilkillki: EDUCATION.

Table 21. Distribution of tin present list (1915 t6) f professional and technical and women's colleges with respect to tin iitc of their opening.
Tai. i. k l"j. li'-ii factions to different lines of higher education in th t nited States each fifth year, 1871 ."'"-.
Dates 1910 1871.
Higher fl,303,431 1,101 .".- .734 92,372 21' I IKK)
Theol 1.4'.
i l 028 1,89 1. 123,812 i 923,831 681
Medical chool i.
i 12,661,076 506 i Jin 183,"
rnal
M'tl'H I i. 3; 147, 112 000 ' In 1914 I I iin 1014law Ktaool Hinting to! In 1913, 189,453; lii 1015 In 1908 lav ' s. 000 in 1908 theol ' 13,271,480.

Considering the stead) decline in strictlj sectarian theology 1111- n l: l th i. r t i tin- i- ri.-1;11 decline in religious Bead, irifis t theological Bcho e been i i all the "i here.

The column f L-ift- to medical Bchooli ihowi the growth that lie taken place in medical science bj well us In medical education through this period.

The tame Is, "f course, no! true of the n log column In the absolute both theological and medical education have prospered Both rise erj slowk from the start, with slight advantage in favor of theological education down to 1890, and with this advantage slowly increasing from 1S90 to 1909, alter which medical education leaps far ahead.

Philanthropy, speaking now in relative terms, very definitely began to turn away from theology about 1890, and soon after to look with slightly more favor upon medical education. In the last decade these tendencies have become marked.

Turning again to Table 22 one is struck first by the immediate and liberal notice which philanthropists gave to the land-grant colleges and schools of science. The last column of the table is interesting in itself, and more so in comparison with the column showing gifts to medical schools. It is apparent here that society began to call a halt on apprenticeship methods of learning medicine before it did the same for law. Law has tended to remain much more a business than a profession, while the opposite is true of medicine and theology.

Taking these data from the Reports of the United States Commissioner of Education as a rough general picture of the educational philanthropy of this period, for it is dependable as such, one is impressed with the large contribution which has been made; with the apparent regularity or dependability of such sources of income; with the size, in the absolute, of the permanent sources which are thus being built up, but with the relative decline in such resources when all higher institutions of education are considered; with the relative increase in the amount of gifts to establish professorships; with the recent tendency toward increase in gifts to cover current expenses; with the regularity with which one-third to one-fifth of all gifts have gone to plant and equipment; with the rise, both relative and absolute, in the gifts to medical schools; with the corresponding decline in gifts to schools of theology; and with the relatively slow increase in gifts to schools of law.

STATUS OF EDUCATION AMONG ALL THE OBJECTS OF PHILANTHROPY.

Another source of data covering almost the last quarter century, and so almost half the period under discussion, is that contained in the Appleton and International Yearbooks and the World's Almanac. In these annuals there have been published the most complete available lists of all gifts of 5,000 and over, together with the object for which each was given. For some of the years these gifts have been classified under the following five heads: Educational institutions; charities; religious organizations; museums, galleries, public improvements; and libraries. Where they were not so classified the writer has been able to make such a classification with reasonable accuracy. In addition the gifts were also recorded as having been made by gift or by bequest, so that this classification was also possible. In these data, then, there is a valuable addition to the general description of philanthropy just presented.

PIIII. ANTIIKMI'Y IX AMI'. RH'AX HIGHER I: i r ' TTON.

Table 23. Distribution of the gifts and bequests recorded in the Appleton and New Jnurnatio-nal Yearbook and the World's Almanac, 1898-1916.

1 Matninadrquatc.

This total column gives ratlin forceful evidence of the Large part of the world's wrk thai is being done by philanthropy. Through these 24 yean the range Is from- to 764 millions of dollars, with an average of nearly 126 millions. In 1915 it; th entire cosl of public education In New York t'iiy was i,010,424, and thai tor Chicago was 28,604,584. in this same year the total outlay for public education In the State of New York, which bad the largesl of nil our State budgets for schools, was 68,761,125, while thai for the United

States was bul 640,717,058. again, the total Inco f all universities, col leges, and technological schools reporting to the United States Commissioner ducarjon In this year was 113,850348. f the buge gifts summarized in the table are flowing annually Ave channels Indicated, we may see from these comparisons the large forces thai constantly to determine the character of the Institutions of edn n. charity, and to on in considering the nun total of all benefactions, three questions deserve con on i li t, whal Is the relative po Itlon of education among the objects of these gifts; second, with whal degree of regularity io thea ome thai is, bow dependable b resource does this make for education; and, third, bow large a contribution is this pj educationi incidentally, there is Interest, too, in the tame que tlon rdlng gifts to other obj iaii. v to Libraries and museums, since th e play a direcl pan In the education of the i pie.

The flm i tlon Is readily answered by Table '." ". from which it will be :, that up to 1018 education was receiving annaall from 18 to 78 per ru of these gifts, with a median of 18 per cent When the figures for L816 are tided, and the totals taken for the 24 yeai period, It can be stated thai education has received approximately 34 per cent of all gifts for the past 24 years. Or, leaving out 1916, as obviously influenced by war charity, education received 43 per cent of all gifts of 5,000 or over in the United States.

The second question, how dependable is this source of income for education, may also be answered by this table, from which it is obvious that from year to year there have been wide variations. Consequently, an average or a median is not a full statement of the history of these benefactions, but the relative status of each of these recipients by years must be considered, and a number of points stand out. First, the facts about variability. What is true of education is true of the other objects. Second, giving to education gradually increased from 1893 to 1906, after which it declined to 1915 and 1916 to a point distinctly lower than the 1893 mark. At the same time the gifts to charity, which roughly maintain their 1893 status down to 1907, make a rise that is even sharper than is the decline in gifts to education. Gifts to religion have been quite variable, but show a general decline from the beginning to the end of the period. Practically the same statement can be made with respect to gifts to museums, galleries, and public improvements, with the exception that the variability is greater. The gifts to libraries show a very definite and regular decline from 1893 to 1916. It follows, then, that charity is education's great competitor, and we may be fairly sure that wars, famines, earthquakes, and other great disasters which appeal to human sympathy for help will be costly to education. The more recent rise in gifts to charity is partly accounted for by the Balkan and the World War and to several great earthquakes and fire disasters.

The third question, how large a help is this to education, is answered in Table 24, where the gifts to education and to libraries are set down beside the figures showing the total annual income to higher education in the United States. The annual income of higher education is used here merely as a convenient basis for measuring the amounts of the benefactions. From this we are able to see what the extent of philanthropy in education really is. To these educational benefactions might with some propriety be added those to libraries.

There is one other item of interest here, brought out in the last two columns of Table 23, viz., the extent to which these benefactions have preceded or followed the death of the donor. In 13 of the 23 years covered by the data a greater per cent has come by direct gift. Summing up the 23 years, the figures are 64 per cent by gift and 36 per cent by bequest. If 1916 is omitted, the figures are: Gifts, 59 per cent and bequests 41 per cent. The lowest per cent of gifts for any year was 17 in 1894 and the highest was 83 in 1906.

Table 24. Total benefactions to all forms of education in the United States, the total income for higher education in the United States as reported by the United States Commissioner of Education, and gifts to libraries.

Years.

1916. 1915. 1914. 1913. 1912. 1911. 1910. 1909. 1908.

Benefactions to all forms of education. 1 572,012,619 35,354,338 90,741,210 57,601,997 35,207,907 01, s79,296 61,283,182 46,122,241 36,552,039

Total income of higher education. 1 133,627,211 11 299,296 109,590,855 104,514,095 94,672,441 80,438,987 76, ft50,969 66,790,924

Benefactions to libraries. 1 2,717,450 jit;. oik) 1,881,000 2,162 2,112.000 1,942,500 1,911, IKi) 3,01. 834,500 1 From yearbooks above cited.

From Reports of the United States Commissioner of Education.

Tabi. k 24. Total benefaction to all forms of education, etc. Continued.

To the general picture then we may add, from trie facts brought out here, that the general Impressions gained from the data of the United States Com missioner's reports are reinforced at several points. Compared with the cost Of education In the country, these t, dl'ts are of reat consideration. Second. they have been, and there is reason to believe thai they will continue to be, a dependable resource. Third. I here is a definite decline in the amount of th(jriftn. which, however, seems to be explained by a corresponding rise in irifts to charity charity so obviously demanded by the greal catastrophes of the years of this decline, in addition, there is a decline in pifts to religion, to public Improvements, and to libraries. With the exception of gifts to libraries. which have slightly declined in absolute amount, these declines are only relative, as may be seen from column three in Table 24. What should have caused this lessening of gifts to libraries is not evidenl from these figures. Carnegie's gifts extend from about 1881, and reports show no special decline in his gifts until very recently.

PHILANTHROPE M "HE OLDER COLLEGES.

Turning again to Tables ". i. and; for a more Intensive study of pbilan throphy as it affected three of our old colonial colleges, we are able to follow the tendencies through the present period.

Brief! stated, It maj be noted that during this period do state support was received; that, looked at from any angle, the amounts of gifts have more than kepi pace with their former record; thai at llar ard and Columbia the earlier tendency to place a condition upon the gifts has continued, while at ale the opposite has been true; and that glftc for permanent endowment shon a rela ii e decline al Harvard and rale through this period, while at Columbia such gifts-': popular than al Harvard, but inmo pi. pular than at Sale.

or the conditional gifts, it may be said thai the " pious and indigent youth ' has continued to fare less well throughout 'bis period; that gifts for scholar' ships and fellowships have become more popular; thai relatively (not in absolute amount i then-has been ii decline in gifts for professorships, except nt Columbia; and thai a still sharper relative decline in gifts to libraries has appeared As t" the form of gift, there u no special tendency anywhere toward gifts or bequests, excepl possible al ".-11. where bequests have increased.

i rerywbere in these older institutions there is evidence of remarkable rowtb Harvard is now well Into the last quarter of its third century, and Columbia beyond the middle ol ond century, There have been do more rapidly changing centuries in history than these. Surely these facts show that educational institutions founded and maintained by philanthropy can keep step with the passing years. If the " dead hand " had lain heavily upon these institutions, they would scarcely have maintained this rate of growth, either in toto or in the special lines here represented.

PHILANTHROPY IN COLLEGES OF THE EARLY NATIONAL PERIOD.

1. NEW LINES OF DEVELOPMENT.

In Chapter IV was described the work of philanthropy in a number of colleges which were founded during the early national period. Several new lines of development were begun in those years, notable among which were the beginnings of separate colleges for women, manual labor colleges, and separate schools of theology. It will be the purpose here to carry forward the study of several of those institutions.

It was said there that the philanthropy of that period was in the main directed by the various churches, and that in point of method the new colleges of those days originated and grew very much as did the colleges of the early colonial times.

2. AMHERST AS AN EXAMPLE OF THE COLLEGES OF LAST PERIOD.

Fairly complete data for Amherst College are presented in Tables 11 and 25. In Table 11 the Amherst data already discussed 3 have been carried forward to 1890. From this may be noted a continuance of most of the tendencies that had prevailed before the Civil War. The State did nothing more for the college, but the average annual income from gifts gradually increased. Most of the gifts were for a specified purpose, and among these, scholarships, professorships, and the library fared well. For some years after the Civil War the gifts were made immediately available, but endowments were favored from 1876 to 1890. The subscription method of obtaining gifts falls into disuse or nearly so, and as was true from the beginning, most of this income was by direct gift rather than by bequest.

In Table 25 is presented Amherst's income from " tuition and student fees," from " productive funds," and from " benefactions." This table covers the period 1895 to 1916, inclusive, at 4-year intervals, and brings out several interesting points. First, the amount from gifts fluctuates from year to year, roughly increasing up to the beginning of the World War and then declining. Income from tuition has also varied, but shows a substantial increase to the present, and income from permanent endowment funds has grown regularly, having more than doubled during the 22 years covered by the table.

Table 25. Income of Amherst College each fourth year, as reported by the United States Commissioner of Education.

PHILANTHROPE IN AMI.1UCAN HIGIIKi: EDUCATION.

From tlic. se facta ii is clear that if the college does not expand too rapidly, it will very boob be on a remarkably Bound basis.

3. THEOLOGICAL INSI1II rioNS.

The growth of Amhersl is somewhat paralleled by that of Andover Theo cal Seminary, the early history of which lias already been discussed. 4 Referring again to Table 12, it will be seen that alter the Civil War, and down to 1890. Andover continued to receive contributions to her permanent funds, and that in increasing amounts. The details of the. se endowments are net all given in the table, but enough is shown to indicate that professorships, scholarships, and the library fared well.

According to reports of the United states Commissioner of Education, the total amount of Andover's permanent funds in L872 was 550,000. With some fluctuations these funds have gradually increased to more than Sspi. utmt in 1915. As early as 1852 these funds were furnishing an annual income of.000. By 1889 this bad grown to 55,000, and it is recorded' that this was tin- entire income of the school for the year.

IP-re. then, is a theological school, founded in 1807, which has slowlj built up an endowment fund that makes it virtually independent 4. WOMEN'S colleges.

As we have already seen," Mount Eolyoke College was one of the pioneer institutions devoted to the hiuditm- education of women. The school was founded and became well established in the second quarter of last century. The following tables will show something of its financial career since the close of the early nal tonal period.

Up to 1875 practically do permanenl endowmenl funds had been accumulated.

The scl i bad in a very real sense been on trial 1 as a new philanthropic social project That it fully proved its worth and received a large social sanction is shown by the figures of Table 26.

Column i of this table shows the total amount of permanenl funds possessed by the college at Intervals of five years from 1st:, to 1915. n 1875 the colli pos essed a permanenl fund of 50,000. in 1915 this had grown to near a million and a half dollars.

Table 26. Total endoioment, ttni income, and sources of iwmu- fur Mount Holyoki College at Intervals o) n years, t875 .".

Hep floe. is1 '

S.-r B, 4.", ff 'A BoatoD papm rafo "I tfl publish Ml ui I, Yon'n itfctcmabta In bohnlf of the college iin,.-. kim for. i adyfrtnInt:. Stow.-, Hint, of lioUBl BolyoK Bem.,." "-1., 1887 (P 41.

It will be seen that permanent funds are rapidly assuming a larger and larger share in the annual income of the college, the main sources of which are also shown in this table. In 1875 the school received 3,000 from the income on permanent funds and 45,000 from student fees. In 1915 permanent funds produced 50,820 and tuition amounted to 114,643. This shows even more clearly what was mentioned above, and just what we have seen to be true of Andover and of Amherst, viz, that the rate of growth in income from permanent funds is greater than is the rate of growth in income from other sources. If this rate continues, it will not be many decades before philanthropy will have produced a college for women that will not be dependent upon student fees and that in spite of an extremely modest financial beginning.

No small part of Mount Holyoke's permanent funds are devoted to the general endowment of the college. The growth of this general fund, together with the permanent fund for scholarships, is shown in Table 27.

Table 27. Growth of ttco of Mount Holyoke's permanent funds, that for general purposes and that for scholarships. 1

Date.

Before 1875.

1876-1880. 1881-1885. 1886-1890. 1891-1895. 1896-1900.

Gifts to permanent fund for

General purposes.

4,640 25,000 50,792 164,134 185,000

Scholarships.

26,666 7,000 22,500 10,000 19,000 43,500

Date.

1901-1905. 1906-1910. 1911-1915.

Total

Gifts to permanent fund for

General purposes.

223,363 5,500 432,750 1,091,179

Scholarships.

14,000 19,500 56 314 218,480 1 Compiled from catalogues and the president's report.

From this table it appears that these two funds have increased rapidly and that each has reached a position of importance in the support of the college.

5. OBERLIN AN EXAMPLE OF THE MANUAL LABOR COLLEGE.

Oberlin College was another institution of the early national period whose early history has been traced. 8 It was pointed out that Oberlin's attempts at gathering funds for permanent endowment were pretty much a failure before the Civil War. Table 2S furnishes us with a very remarkable sequel, however, to that earlier story of hard times, for since the Civil War Oberlin has made progress quite similar to that noted above for Amherst, Andover, and Mount Holyoke.

It is not only in Oberlin's total, however, but in the purposes for which these totals were given that we see the large value of her endowment. This the table makes clear through a period of almost a half century.

Tabu 28.- Distribution of Oberun'a permanent funds, received bu oift and bequest, 18SS 1915' 1 Data for this table were compiled from the Oberhn General Catalogue, 1S33-190S. and the yuinquennial Catalogue for 1916.

1 Of the total amount of benefactions for this purpose to 19os. "1 per a ut was received as direct (24 percent by bequest, ami 25 per cent by endowment canvasses. Nearly 26 prr cent of it was foi the endowment of religious and theological Instruction and 1 per cent to instruction in natural and physical aces.

I 'ft tie total amount given for the endowment of scholarships during these years, 22 per cent was received by bequests, nearly 5 percent came from churches, and: per cent from different classes ol alumni. About 14 per rent of it was for thase entering missionary work or those who were children of missionaries, more Hum."", per cent was for indigent self-supporting students, 8 per cent for colored students, and 16 per cent for girls.

Some details concerning the growth of the professorship fund- arc added in Table 29. Prom these fuels it appears that slightly more than half of the total of these funds was built ap by subscription methods, approximately one-fourth by gift and the same by bequest

Tabi k ". ' f'. innoutit. nid. sourer f each endowed professorship at Oberlin College.

Considering th ir colleges ai falrlj representative ol 'hi- philanthropic foundations of the earlj national period, we maj aaj of their development e the i ii w'ai thai in ait cases this bai been a period of rapid growth, The period of experimentation seems to have passed about war times, ami tie-.- college to bave i d accepted as worthy of the full confidence of pin lanthropy, permanent fiin. is began to accumulate, slowly at Aral and then ut : m n- rate, till now all lime a-up-l anl ial income fr luCO fumk

At the present rate of growth, and with no more than normal expansion, these colleges will in time become practically independent of income from other sources. The endowment funds of these colleges are in large part available for general purposes, though considerable sums have been given for professorships, scholarships, and library.

PHILANTHROPY IN THE COLLEGES OF THIS PERIOD.

Down to 1865 practically every college had begun its existence with very small funds, usually with little or no real endowment, and had had to pass through a long financial struggle before it had won a clientage sufficient to guarantee its future. During the period here under discussion colleges continued to be founded on that same basis. Drury College began in poverty in 1873 and remained poor until 1892, when a gift of 50,000 laid the foundation of her present endowment of over a quarter of a million. Carleton College, chartered in 1867, began with 20,000 received from the citizens of Northfield and 10,000 received from the Congregational Churches of the State. In 1915 this college possessed endowment funds of almost a million dollars. Washburn College, chartered in 1865, was started by small gifts from the Congregational Churches, but by 1915 had developed an endowment of over 360,000. These are but three from the many well-known illustrations of this type.

1. THE PRIVATELY ENDOWED UNIVERSITY A NEW TYPE.

In addition to this type, however, we see the beginning of a new era in educational philanthropy an era in which a great and independently endowed university could spring into existence almost at once from the gifts of a single benefactor.

Such schools did not have to go to the public and beg for funds, nor await any sort of social sanction. They secured their charters as corporations, erected their buildings, called together their faculties, organized their curricula, and opened their doors to students. They start, therefore, as educational and philanthropic, and we might also say, social experiments. Can such financially powerful corporations be trusted to keep faith with America's educational, economic, religious, and social ideals was the question in many minds at that time.

An examination of the charters, articles of incorporation, and other foundation documents of these institutions should reveal something of their own conception of what their function was to be. Accordingly the following excerpts from these sources are presented: 1. EDUCATIONAL AIMS.

The charter of Vassar College was issued in 1861. Section 2 of this charter declares it to be the object and purpose of the corporation " To promote the education of young women in literature, science, and the arts."

A fuller statement is to be found in Matthew Vassar's address to the trustees of the college, delivered on February 26, 1861, in which he says: I wish that the course of study should embrace at least the following particulars: The English language and its literature; other modern languages; the ancient classics, as far as may be demanded by the spirit of the times: the mathematics, to such an extent as may be deemed advisable; all the branches of natural science, with full apparatus, cabinets, collections, and conservatories for visible illustrations; anatomy, physiology, and hygiene, with practical reference to the laws of health of the sex; intellectual philosophy; the elements of political economy; some knowledge of the Federal and State Constitutions fs PHILANTHROPY IN AMERICAN HIGHER EDUCATION.

and laws; moral science, particularly as bearing on the filial, conjugal, and parental relations; aesthetics,; is treating of the beautiful in nature and art. and in be illustrated by an extensive gallery of art; domestic economy, prae-dly taught, so far as possible, in order to prepare graduates readily to become skillful housekeepers; last, and most Important of all, the daily, systematic reading and study f the Holy Scriptures as the only and ali-sulhcient rule of Christian faith and practice.

Cornell's charter, granted in 1S65, says, in section 3:

The leading object of the corporation hereby created shall be to teach such branches of learning as are related to agriculture and the mechanical arts, incndlng military tactics; in order to promote the liberal and practical education of the industrial classes in the several pursuits and professions in life. But such other branches of science and knowledge may be embraced in the plan of instruction and Investigation pertaining to the university as the trustees may deem useful and proper. 10 In addition to this statement from the charter, we have the following words from Ezra Cornell, the founder: u I hope we have laid the foundation of an institution which shall combine practical with liberal education, I desire that this shall prove to be the beginning of an institution which shall furnish better means for the culture of all men, of every calling, of every aim; training them to be more useful in their relations to th e State, and to better comprehend their higher and holier relations to their families and their God.

Finally, I trust we have laid the Foundation of a university "an Institution where any person can find instruction in any study."

Johns Hopkins Bays in his will: I do hereby give, devise, and bequeath all the rest of my real and personal estate to be held, used, and applied by such corporation in. for. and to its corporate purposes in accordance with the provision of its existing charier of incorporation, etc"

In this brief and formal certificate of incorporation of Augu-r 24, 1867, " e find the general declaration of purpose to be thai of "Organizing a university for the promotion Of education: n the State of. Maryland," etc."

These general ideas of the purpose of Johns Hopkins University are made a bit mor 1c in the inaugural address of the flrsl president in which he lays down 12 principles fairly well expressed in the following br. rpts:"

l. All sciences are worthj of promotion, etc 2 Religion has nothing to fear from science, and vice versa.

3 Remote utilltj Is Quite as worthy to be thoughl ol as Immediate ad vanta: I i As it is impossible for any university to encourage with equal freedom ail branches (learning, a selection musl be made by enlightened governors, and thai-diction musl depend on the requirements and Bdenciea of a given people in a given period.

5. Teachers and pupils musl be allowed great freedom In their method of work.

i,, his next ral principles be lass emphaala upon the Importance of a broad libera culture tor ail students; upon research tor professors upon the infiiion; re earch upon Instruction, and vice feroa; points out that honors must be bestowed sparingly arid benefits freely; and says that a university is low growth and ery liable to fall into nil-.

i,, i,. r. inm. Monro, unci Bilght, Kii7j itii Basettoa, appeadla n.

Oonu 111 B i oonder'i address in the unci, miii. f President White u i " s. t" Hiorrnpny of Mi a 1 Barnes ft Co., 1884 p 189 ff ihne iioj. kinx i Diversity Charter, ftrtracts of Will, Oflfoera ad By-Laws. n iti 1874 pntii. Md irltn eabseaneal umadaeeats in mi University ttfvihit for i9is-in. A(i(in w ut ttte laaafuratlon ol Daalel C oilman, a Pre Idenl of Johiib iiopkina University, liaiamvrt., l- I

The founding grant of Leland Stanford Junior University declares that it is " Its object to qualify its students for personal success and direct usefulness in life."

And further: Its purposes, to promote the public welfare by exercising an influence in behalf of humanity and civilization, teaching the blessings of liberty regulated by law, and inculcating love and reverence for the great principles of government as derived from the inalienable rights of man to life, liberty, and the pursuit of happiness.

In addition to work of instruction, th university was designed " to advance learning, the arts, and sciences."

In the University of Chicago certificate of incorporation we find the aim of the foundation expressed in section 2 as follows:

To provide, impart, and furnish opportunities for all departments of higher education to persons of both sexes on equal terms; to establish and maintain a university in which may be taught all branches of higher learning.

Such are the educational aims of these institutions as they were conceived by the founders.

2. RELIGIOUS AIMS.

The religious emphasis is shown to some extent in these same documents.

Vassar's charter makes no reference to religion, but Mr. Vassar, in the address above quoted, does. In addition to the reference to religion in the above quotation, he says:

All sectarian influences should be carefully excluded; but the training of our students should never be intrusted to the skeptical, the irreligious, or the immoral.

Cornell's charter makes specific reference to religion, as follows:

Sec. 2. But at no time shall a majority of the board be of any one religious sect or of no religious sect.

Sec. 3. And persons of every religious denomination shall be equally eligible to all offices and appointments.

In Johns Hopkins' brief charter no reference is made to religion, but in President Gilman's address, as above quoted, we can see that questions of religion were to fix no limitations in the life of the university at any point.

Leland Stanford's foundation grant as amended in October, 1902, says:

The university must be forever maintained upon a strictly nonpartisan and nonsectarian basis.

The charter of the University of Chicago says:

Sec. 3. At all times two-thirds of the trustees and also the president of the university and of said college shall be members of regular Baptist Churches in this particular this charter shall be forever unalterable.

No other religious test or particular religious profession shall ever be held as a requisite for election to said board or for admission to said university or for election to any professorship or any place of honor or emolument in said corporation, etc.

Such aims as these could not have been expressed in earlier college charters. The idea of educating young women in the sciences; the idea of connecting science as taught in the college with the work of the farmer and mechanic; the laboratory method of teaching; the idea of investigation and research as a university function; the slight general references to and the broad liberality in matters of religion; these things could not have been written into the foundation documents of our colonial colleges. There is a marked contrast between the general tone and the actual ideas and ideals expressed here and those shown from colonial charters in Table 1 above.

The uew education is strong!; suggested in almost every line of those docu-ments, and a careful analysis of the conditions placed upon the foundation ts would show thai trerj little Is to be subtracted from the showing which the above quotations make . Mr. Rockefeller demanded that the Baptist ESducation Hoard Bbould raise sim, mx) to imt with his ift of set m 1,000. his uift to become a permanent endowment for currenl expenses. The conditions of his next several large jzifts were quite as simple.

. Matthew Vassar placed in the hands of his trustees securities worth 400,000 with which to build a seminars and college for women. He explained what his notion of such a college was and then very modestlv advised the hoard as to future use of the funds.

Mr. Cornell bad to meet the demands not alto-ether reasonable of the State of New York, and those of the national land-rant act of 1862 before he could give 500,000 to build a university.

These are typical. These great fortunes were to build and endow a " college " or a ' university,"' as the rase mi-ht be. ami no narrow limitations were placed upon the use of the gifts to those ends. With such large initial funds available, it is obvious thai these institutions are in a position to reject an. subsequent gift that does not meet the essential purposes for which the BChoOls were founded. The aims laid down in their charters can be carried out without help if necessary. 11; " 111 It is especially noteworthy, therefore, that in no case has society failed to accept (lie lotindat ion in the right spirit. Almost from the start the people made these projects their own, as was evidenced l the con tributions which vers soon began to llou into their treasuries from outside

Bources.

3. IVCKS oi i: iav CONDITIOHA GIFTS.

Vassar College.- Vassar College was founded in 1861 and was opened to students in iscr. Mr. Yassar's first gift was 408, In 1864 he added a gift of 20,000, for an art collection, and in 1868, by bis will, be canceled a 75,000 debt for the college, and added 275,000 to establish a lectureship fund, a

Students' aid fund, a lihrarv and art cabinet fund, and a repair fund. The : important gift t" come to Vassar from the outside was in isti when a.1 i'o gave 6,000 to establish the Fox scholarship. This was soon followed by two other gifts for scholarships and in 1878 i a-ift of 6,000, and iii 1882 bj am. t her of 3,000, both for scholarships."

In lsT'. t two of the founder's nephews agreed I" build a laboratory Of ehem ', and phs-ics; in addition to which Matthew Vassar. jr. gave 50,000 for scholarships and 40,000 for twO professorships In Is; mi an endowment fund 100,000 U as raised by rabscrlptlons. 11

Andrew ii white, iii tits Autobiography, Vol. I, p 118, quota the following atatement from. i trn I f Jobni Hopklna t d! " Wo at leaal bave tbla In oui favor; wo can follow out onr own coaci ind com of what la beat; wo bave no i it of oboj Ing tin- Injunction! of an) leglelature, it" belief! of anj religion body, or the rlamora i, fan-, pre w. oe free to do what we ran 11 j believe beat a ilowlj and In aucb mannei

UH We sit III."

'in accepting omc of thctre icholarablp tbe college t–ot, il itacjf for all tine to edn n k'trl on eacb of tbe foundation! That w. Ic when money waa wortb 7 pet. and 11 boj feli. hi. ami iin . f-ii'ti edu. Mtii. ii n "" acta; ii' Uabilll 1.-. in place ol i el Tbla, however, h. i no fault of philanthropy, tnt due rather to short Igbted management on the t rt (the college, Buch management wna Dot, however, without precedent. See illai iiaoliui of Olwillii Keii. iiur iii. p ic wore tiik.-u froui Halloa mid 11ni iit., i. o,. in. i from Proetdaut'a Ke-imru and iataloguea.

This covers practically all the gifts to Vassar during its first 25 years of work. Certainly the conditions named have been in line with the main purposes of the founder.

Cornell University. At Cornell University, founded in 1865, we have a somewhat different situation. The half million dollar gift of the founder was very thoroughly hound to fulfill certain conditions laid down by the State legislature. 18 The university started and grew against serious opposition of almost every sort, and almost immediately gifts began to be received.

In 1871 Henry W. Sage gave 250,000 to establish and endow a women's college; John Mcgraw erected the Mcgraw Building, at a cost of about 100,000; Hiram Sibley presented a building and equipment for the college of mechanic arts at a cost of over 50,000; President White built the President's House, at a cost of some 60,000; and Dean Sage endowed the chapel which had been built by a gift of Henry W. Sage. These are typical of many other early gifts which produced a phenomenally rapid growth of the university. 19

John Hopkins University. Johns Hopkins opened its doors in 1876, having been chartered in 1867. Almost immediately its large foundation began to be supplemented by gifts and bequests. In his will, dated February 26, 1876, Dr. Henry YV. Baxley left 23. S36 to found a medical professorship. In the same year a small gift was received for a scholarship, and this was followed by several others during the next few years. Large and important book collections, including a large German law library for Heidelberg, were contributed to the library very soon after it was opened, and two 10,000 fellowships were contributed in 1887. Numerous small gifts are also recorded, but these are fully typical of the conditional gifts to Johns Hopkins during her first two decades. 211

Chicago University. Among the early gifts to the University of Chicago after it was chartered in 1890 was a site for the college by Marshall Field and a million-dollar gift from Mr. Rockefeller, 800,000 of the latter to be used as a permanent fund for the support of nonprofessional graduate instruction and fellowships, 100,000 to be used as a permanent fund for the endowment of theological instruction in the divinity school of the university, and 100,000 to be used in the construction of buildings for the divinity school. In 1891 the trustees of the William B. Ogden estate began proceedings which ended in a gift of nearly 600,000 for the Ogden Graduate School of Science. In 1893 Silas B. Cobb gave a 150,000 recitation building, and in this same year three other large gifts for buildings were received. Numerous other gifts, such as an astronomical observatory, a physical laboratory, a chemistry building. an oriental museum, followed within a few years, as also did large sums for endowment.

Leland Stanford Junior University. At Leland Stanford Junior University, opened in 1891 on the largest initial foundation gift yet made to an American institution of higher learning, numerous valuable gifts were made to the library and museum from the start. The half-million dollar jewel fund for the endowment of the library was the gift of Mrs. Stanford in 1905. Other large gifts from Thomas Welton Stanford restored the museum, which had been destroyed by the earthquake in 1906, and added an art museum and a 18 By the charter the university was made subject to visitation of the regents of the University of New York, and the trustees were made personally liable for any debt above 50,000. It also made the founding gift of Mr. Cornell absolutely unconditional.

18 For these facts, see President White's Autobiography, and W. T. Hewett's Cornell University, a History, Vol. Ill, Appendix.

20 See A List of Gifts and Bequests Received by the John Hopkins University, 1876-1891, Baltimore, 1892.

valuable art collection. Several prize scholarship, fellowship, and lectureship funds were also among the early gifts.

We may say, then, that these institutions did receive gifts from the outside, and that very soon after they were founded. We may say that the conditions of these gifts were unquestionably in accord with the essential aims set forth in the charters of the schools. In other words, these projects met the real test and passed it, and having received society's sanction they have joined the ranks of Harvard. Yale, Columbia, Oberlin, Amherst, and the long list of institutions which these names suggest.

4. ANALYSIS OF GIFTS TO TWO UNIVERSITIES OF THIS GH001.

It is possible to add to this description something of the financial history of two of these universities. Tables 30 and 31 give us a fairly complete account of the income to the University of Chicago and to Cornel! University at Intervals of five years down to 1915. An one of the columns of these tables is instructive. All point to the phenomenal growth of these onlvei sities. The income from tuition shows the rapid growth of the student bodies, and when compared with the column showing the total income it is seen that throughout Cornell's history tuition has furnished from one-fourth to one-seventh of the total annual income, while at the University of Chicago this percentage is from one-third to one-fifth. The income from productive funds in both tables shows a steady and rapid increase almost from the start. and at Cornell has furnished from two to six and even nine times the income produced by tuition.

The gifts column in Table 31 shows that gifts have become, subsequently to 1S0O, an extremelj Important and dependable source of income, it should be added that an examination of the treasurer's reports shows that a large percentage of these uh fts to Cornell have been going into the permanent funds of the university.

In Table 30 we have a further analysis of the benefactions to the University of Chicago after lrx'u"), from which we are able to see the extent to which gifts are being received for enlargement of plant, tor endowment, and for current expeo pectively, from which it Is evident that a very large percentage of all gifts go into the permanent funds.

Tabu 30. Inconu niveraity o Chicago at 5-year interval (ruin i: o to r."ir."

Table 31. Financial exhibit of income of Cornell University at five-year intervals from 1865 to 1915. 1 1 Data to 1904 from Hewett's Cornell University, and subsequent to 1904 from Reports of the United States Commissioner of Education.

From these figures it is evident that the scale upon which these institutions were founded has been fairly maintained as their scale of growth. Chicago's income from permanent funds is furnishing an increasing proportion of her annual income, while the opposite appears to be true of Cornell. The latter is explained by the fact that Cornell has in recent years been receiving relatively large annual appropriations from the State, the city, and the United States. What we have noted above regarding the endowment funds of the colonial and early national colleges, then, is equally true of these younger institutions. They are rapidly building up a source of support that will, under normal expansion, make them independent.

If we ask regarding the further conditions placed upon these vast gifts to higher education, we have'but to read over the lists published in the yearbooks, in magazines, and in official university publications to see that they are rarely out of line with the main lines of growth in the institution receiving them. More than half of Cornell's permanent funds belong to the general funds of the university or to some one of the schools or departments."

Of the great foundations of this period then we may say: Financially they are practically independent from the start; each is, in the main, the gift of one man; their charters grant them' almost unlimited freedom to become anything they may choose to call college or university; they are very definitely nonsectarian and nonpolitical, but one, Chicago, is definitely fostered by a church; they cultivate liberality in matters of religion; they stress original research as a professorial function; and, in the face of real opposition in some cases, as well as the natural tendency to distrust such large corporations, the gifts they have received from the start show that they have been accepted by the public as fully as have the most ancient or most religious foundations of the past. All are rapidly building up permanent endowment funds which promise a large degree of financial independence in the future, and, judged by our best standards, all are not only fully law-abiding, but each in its own way is exercising wide leadership in the field of higher education.

PHILANTHROPY THROUGH RELIGIOUS EDUCATION SOCIETIES.

As explained in Chapter III, religious education societies arose very early in the last century in response to a growing demand for trained ministers, n A foil list of these funds with date and amount of each, and with fairly complete statement of conditions controlling the use of their income, is published In the annual report of the treasurer for 1915-16.

philanthropy in amii: iax fflgHEB EDUCATION.

which demand the colleges were failing to meet. They organize! and were chartered as corporations to aid in the education of young men for this calling. They operated mainly by direct aid to the student, though in some cases grants wen- made to colleges. Mosl of the societies did some work of this kind, even going so far as to found colleges in some instances. 12

Mosl of these societies survived the period of the Rebellion and have continued, separately or in combination, to carry on this work to the present time. Many other societies have also been organized, several new ones having appeared very recently. The old methods of assistance have continued in force, and permanent endowment funds have in several cases grown to Importance, and it is plain that the Influence of these organizations is becoming greater. At present they are organized on denominational lines, though originally man; of them were not so.

1. THE AMERICAN EDUCATION SOCIETY.

Something of the extent Of their service to higher education may be seen from the following tables, which are typical of the best work that is being done by these societies. Table 32 shows the annual income of the American education Society, the number Of Students assisted, the amount of permanent funds possessed, the total annual grant to colleges, and. for a few years, the number of colleges receiving these grants. The first two columns are a continuation of columns one and two in Table 14.

Table 32- Financial statistics o the Imerioan Education Society at intervals of five years mm t 6ti to 1915.

i illy much is' i ac tdemie than to 5 In thli vf. ir' 18! imed with tii' foi 'in Promotion i- Theok . chartered, and became the Unerii in Collegi and Bducat If we turn to Table

11 we will gee that this society grew rapidly front its in 1815 to ueii into the thirties, after whieh it slowly declined until after 'be Civil War, when it again entered upon period of prosperitj which tinned practically to ibe presenl ilme, In 1 7 1 the American BduCation Society, which had worked mainly by to itudents, was combined with the Society for the Promotion of Col ate and Theological Education in the West, which bad operated bj making grants to collegi Tin- ahifl in emphasis appears in column 4 under "grant!

The rise in income along with the decline in Dumber of s tu dents and colleges aide plained by the fad that Inc. attention has been given to the

Aa-in n tin- western Collegi. founded lluoja 'iieic in

"See i- 60 n.

work of academies, pastorates, and missionary schools. 24 The society has not only prospered, but its total service to education has increased.

2. THE PRESBYTERIAN EDUCATION BOARD.

Table 33 continues for the board of education of the Presbyterian Church the facts shown for that society in Table 14. In addition, this table shows the number of churches from which contributions were received, and the maximum amount and the total amount of aid granted to students.

Table 33. Financial statistics of the Presbyterian Board of Education at intervals of five years. 1 1 Statistics from the 98th An. Rep. of the board, in 1917; the Cumberland Presbyterian Education Society united with this board in 1906; their first joint report is in 1907.

First of all, it will be seen that since 1878 the number of churches contributing to the funds of this society has practically trebled. This increase in the society's clientage has been very gradual, and an examination of the receipts shows that the average contribution per church has remained fairly constant or perhaps increased slightly. If we examine the three last columns of this table we see that its service has also increased. The number of students aided has increased from 296 in 1866 to 1,037 in 1896; then, after a decline for a few years, has risen again to 895 in 1917. During these years the amount of aid per student has fluctuated somewhat but on the whole has declined, while the total of grants has varied somewhat with the number of students aided.

3. METHODIST EPISCOPAL CHURCH BOARD.

The board of education of the Methodist Episcopal Church took definite form in 1S64. Its charter empowered it to aid young men desiring to enter missionary work or the ministry, and to aid biblical or theological schools, as well as universities, colleges, and academies then (1869) under the patronage of the church. No gifts were to be made for buildings and no aid was to be given to any school not then in existence, except " the board shall first have been consulted and shall have approved of the establishment and organization of such institution." " Down to 1908 it has rendered aid to higher education

M See An. Rep. of the Treasurer, 1916.

25 See the original charter of 1S69, published in the 1904 report.

111512 22- entirely by making loans direct to students, for the reason that it had practically no funds for work of a broader scope." Since that time it has, in addition to this, made grants to colleges. Table 34 shows the annual receipts from gifts, the annual outlay in the form of loans to students, the annual grants to institutions, and, for some years, the number of students receiving these loans. From these figures it is evident that this society has made a remarkably rapid growth. From its beginning in 1 7.3 to 1915 the hoard claims to have assisted a total of 2.:'.: ' different students 7 That includes those in the academies and theological schools as well as those in college.

Table 34. Financial statistics of the board of education of the Methodist Episcopal Church, 1868-1915, at intervals of five years?

1 Compiled from annual and quadrennial reports of tin- board.

Table 35. Biennial receipts of tht board of education of tin Evangelical

Lutheran ("hurcii in the United state of America.

I. i. s m; i-i fcAL M m ERA IS CHI IN m no VRD.

in 1886 the hoard of education of the Evangelical Lutheran Church in the Qnlted states of America was organized and baa operated continuously since. Table 86-how-, the resources of the hoard biennially since Its foundation fta method of wort has been that of making contributions to various educational titutions. According to treasurer-' reports, gifts to colleges were sometimes for the "budget" of the school and sometimes for s specific Item, as interest on a debt, special endowment, scholarship, etc For the past decade reports , v iimt at as were regular recipients of aid from this hoard, and it appears from reports to have been rt ble for founding, and o for refusing to found, new Institutions, which together Indicates that it Is in some ipervlalng ag ncy

Be; rion of ihih in ttm annual report! board for 1904.

"An. Sep.,

While it is not possible to state just what proportion of the funds of these societies has gone into higher education, it is clear that all effort has been aimed directly or indirectly at training for the ministry. One has but to glance at the columns, and especially at their totals, to realize that these organizations have meant much to the growth of higher education in this country. The income of the Presbyterian board for 1917 is approximately that of such colleges as Wells and Beloit.

The showing for these four societies or boards is probably typical of the best that is being done by these organizations. Undoubtedly thousands of young men and women have received secondary or collegiate training who would otherwise have received little or no schooling. The ministry has brought many into its service by this means. These societies have saved colleges which were virtually bankrupt. By small gifts they have stimulated much larger ones. They have exercised supervision over colleges under their patronage by refusing aid to those which show no promise. They have by these and other means attempted standardization, and it should be added that the Methodist board began to exercise this influence very early. 28 They have through church pulpits and Sunday schools brought the problems of college education to the attention of a large percentage of our population. More recently coordination of the efforts of these many boards, through the work of the council of church boards of education, is resulting in a more intelligent placement of new foundations. Doubtless we should add that these boards have helped to save denominationalism among churches, whatever that may be worth.

Most of them seem to be worthy aims, if the cost has not been too great. In opposition to this kind of philanthrophy it is sometimes argued that a young man who is put through college by the aid of these boards naturally feels obligated to enter the ministry regardless of the fact that he discovers in the course of his training that he is better fitted for some other calling; that, as a rule, academy students are not in a position to decide upon a vocation; that the scholarship method, unless appointments are based upon ability, is not the best way to stimulate scholarly efforts; and that the cost of administering the funds is too large. 29 It is clear at any rate that these boards are occupying a much stronger position among the churches than formerly. Their supervision is real supervision, when it is possible for them to close up such of their own weaker insti- 28 In 1802 general conferences of the Methodist Episcopal Church authorized a "university senate " to formulate a standard of requirements for graduation to baccalaureate degree in their church schools, and the board was authorized to classify as colleges only such schools as met those requirements. See Appendix to Annual Report for 1892, and for the general conference for 1806, p. 736. The colleges are classified on this basis in the annual reports of the board for 1895.

20 In 1875 approximately 11 per cent of the expenditures of the American College and Education Society was for the cost of administration. The cost of administration for the Methodist board amounted to more than 16 per cent of the total expenditures in 1889, and about 27 per cent in 1915, and the same figure for the Presbyterian board in 1SSS was about 10 per cent. Of course these are only rough figures. The administrative officers are often engaged in ways that are directly useful in the development of higher education. The application of college standards by the administrative officers of the Methodic board is a fair illustration. The making of educational surveys, the gathering and publication of educational information, the vast amounts of correspondence in connection with gifts and loans, and the advice to colleges concerning their educational and financial development, are all illustrations. In a sense these boards are all engaged in propaganda work, the results of which it Is difficult to evaluate.

rations as they may decide are no longer useful. These boards are not only taking a scientific attitude toward this problem, but they are studying their colleges to see what are needed and what are not needed, and are advocating, and in many cases effecting, the close of the superfluous institutions."

6. COUNCIL 01 CHT7BCB BOARDS OF EDUCATION.

There is one feature of this whole movement which seems to promise very great possibilities for good. That is the recent ly organized council of church boards of education. This council was organized In 1911, and has for its purpose a more intelligent cooperation among churches in the building and maintenance of church colleges." Possibly it was the influence of the more powerful philanthropic agencies, together with the growing prestige Of the great privately endowed and State universities, that brought the small church college to realize that its influence was beginning to wane.

This movement toward cooperation is one important outcome of the vigorous discussions of the place of the small college in American higher education. These boards knew many of the weak points in the church college situation and knew that duplication of effort was probably their greatest weakni

At an informal conference of the secretaries of seven church boards of education, held in New York City, February 18, 1911, it was decided that a second conference should be held at which carefully prepared papers should be presented.

Such a conference was held and resulted in the following declaration of principles: (1) A large degree of cooperation between educational boards la practicable and desirable. "Through them we might secure a better geographical distribution Of denominational colleges a proper standardization of institutions," etc. (2) The denominations should offer loyal support to the pub lie-school system. (3) The legitimacy and the absolute necessity of a certain number of denominational academies, occupying strategic positions In territory not fully occupied by the public high schools. (4) There should be a direct ap proacb by the denominations to the problem of religious Instruction at state university centers." The council took permanent form at the conclusion of this meeting and has

Since published annual reports of its work. Several practical steps toward Cooperation between the boards have already been taken, and. though its p i standardizing agency maj remain advisory only, it is in that capacity t i! tence as a philanthropic agency offers substantia promise,

Bl VI M KV M) ("N,, s,, NS.

We may characterize this period In the growth of higher education In America as follow

The que tion of state versus private endowment of higher education has been Fought through and settled favorably to both methods; the church baa con tinned its work of founding small coll.-. ral v. r large Institutions (ill

B new type) have been founded by the fortunes of single individuals 1 arch for support: a Dumber (large foundations, o Bee Etep EM- ' MI EDp Ch., 1910 far lllu 1 Black nun (-. ii.-K'-. 1908; Charles I i lege, ' nivei Itj of the Pacific and Fort tn University, 1911; Mount F nnan College, 1908, are a few of the Met!

uny.

u! ration of the council ih print.! la the Second Annual H i. rt of the Coun rll of Chiir. li I'. n. ir. 1 ' ' a! Ion, s.-.- i ir. i An Etep of Council of ciuirch!" ' i 'i In 1 B America the aim of which is research and general educational stimulus and supervision, have been created; and a new philosophy of education, which has found expression in the organization, administration, and management of our institutions of higher learning, has been worked out.

In opening up new territory to higher education during this period, the State has for the most part done the pioneering, thus reversing the custom of pre-Civil War days, when the church school led the way.

From a general view of the work of philanthropy in higher education, as gathered from the Reports of the United States Commissioner of Education, we have seen that philanthropy has gradually built up a vast fund for the permanent endowment of higher learning; that from this source, together with annual gifts, philanthropy is still bearing decidedly the larger part of the burden of higher education, though the State is assuming a relatively larger portion of this burden each year; and that tuition has covered practically the same percentage of the total annual cost from 1872 to the present. We have seen that, on an average, more than half of all gifts have gone to " permanent endowment and general purposes "; that there is a tendency in recent years for a larger proportion to go into the permanent funds; and that from one-eighth to one-half of the annual gifts have been for the development of the school plant. We have seen that in the seventies and eighties professorships and libraries fared well; that scholarships became increasingly important, and that the indigent never were quite forgotten; and, finally, that the percentage of all gifts that have been made without condition through the years has ranged from 4 to 26 per cent.

From other data we have seen that philanthropy has been almost solely responsible for the development of separate colleges for women, and for theological schools; that it has played a large part in the development of medical schools, and a small part in technical and law schools; and that private enterprise and the State have been almost entirely responsible for the development of schools of dentistry and pharmacy, while the State has been largely responsible for technical schools.

From data in the various annual publications from 1893 to 1915, inclusive, we have seen that education has received 43 per cent of all gifts of 5,000 or over in the United States; that charity is education's largest competitor, with 37 per cent; while " religious purposes " balances with museums and public improvements at approximately 9 per cent each, and libraries at 2 per cent. Roughly, and relatively speaking, we may say that during the first half of this period the amount of gifts for education made a slight gain, since which it has suffered a steady decline. Similarly religious purposes and museums have suffered a substantial though irregular decline from the start, while libraries have made a continuous decline from the first. These changes are in practically all cases only relative.

Among the old colonial colleges we have seen that the entire burden has fallen upon philanthropy and student fees, the States having offered no assistance whatever through this period. In spite of this, gifts have increased greatly. Conditional gifts have become somewhat more popular, but slightly the opposite is true with respect to gifts for permanent funds. Gifts to libraries and to indigent students have declined, while professorships have remained approximately as before.

In the colleges of the early national period we see the same rapid growth of funds from philanthropy as noted for the older institutions. In the colleges of this period the rapid growth of permanent funds is especially noticeable, and, further, the larger portion of these gifts are for the general fund. With this growth of general endowment have also prospered professorships, scholarships, and libraries.

As to the colleges of this period, no study was made of what we think of as the small church college. The work of this character is undoubtedly Important, but there is little If anything new coming from it. The real contribution of the period is the group of large foundations. With one or two exceptions these are not church-fostered and not State-fostered institutions us all their ancestors have been. They encourage liberality in religion, they offer the most liberal scientific education for women, they encourage the use of museum and laboratory methods of teaching, and they foster research as a university function.

An examination of the financial history of this typo of institution shows that in all cases they have been promptly taken over by the people and are now among the most important recipients of gifts In this country. Their rate of growth has been very great almost from the start, and all our evidence goes to show that these powerful financial corporations, planted In the midst of small colleges and accepted in some quarters with misgiving, have not only kept faith with earlier social, religious, and educational aims, but, in the readjustment of those aims to our rapidly expanding age, they have shown capacity proportionate to their greal financial power, and what was to some a doubtful experiment is a success

Through this period we have seen the continuation of the work of church boards of education, or religious education societies. These are rapidly iucr, ing in numbers, there being a tendency for each church to have its own hoard. Their work has been conducted along two main lines. They have contributed scholarships either by gift or by loan, and they have made grants to colleges to meet either a general or some special need. Their chief aim has continued to be the development of a trained ministry, though the development of colleges in which all students will be kept in a proper religious atmosphere reels secondary. The evidence presented shows that these societies have prospered. Thej are contributing direel assistance to many hundreds of stu dents every year; they are making grants direct to colleges, grants which. though small, have often been directlj responsible for larger gifts; they have in some measure exercised supervision over the Founding of new schools, over curricula, and finance; ami by their cooperation through the council of church hoards of education the) promise much more for the future.

Chapter V. GREAT EDUCATIONAL FOUNDATIONS.

A NEW PHILANTHROPIC ENTERPRISE.

A type of philanthropic educational enterprise peculiar to the period just discussed is that of the large foundation whose purpose is not alone, nor even primarily, that of teaching but rather that of supplementing and assisting established institutions of education.

One can scarcely read the founding documents of these institutions without being struck first of all with the very wide scope of service which they have undertaken. The Peabody Fund promoted popular education in the South by cooperation with State and local officials. The Jeanes, the Slater, and the Phelps-Stokes Fund have been devoted to the problems of education for negroes. The Carnegie Foundation for the Advancement of Teaching has concerned itself with salaries, pensions, and insurance for college professors. The General Education Board has helped along several of these lines and paid much attention to educational 'investigations, and especially to a more substantial endowment of existing institutions. The Sage Foundation has contributed liberally by investigation, research, and publication.

These foundations, therefore, appear as a really new type of philanthropic enterprise in education, with church education boards as their only possible precedent, and though, as compared with the educational assets of some of our great cities, or with sums which numerous States are utilizing annually, or even with a few of our universities, they are not remarkably large, yet they are large enough to represent very great possibilities, and society can not afford to take them lightly. Can our country assimilate this new enterprise, is a question that might have been asked when Mr. Peabody and his successors began pouring out their millions in the development of this new business, the business of educational philanthropy.

The church college was antagonistic toward the State institutions of higher education when the latter began to grow rapidly into great universities, and they were also
quite skeptical of the great privately endowed universities, lest they might be Godless
schools. The State, the church, and the individual philanthropist were in a fairly real
sense competitors in the field, and it was bul natural that the old pioneer, the church
college, should at first be jealous of what seemed to be its special prerogative. This
rivalry has continued, but it has become increasingly friendly with passing years.

These new foundations, however, do not enter the field as rivals, but. Instead, aim
definitely to supplement and to cooperate with forces already at work. What work will
they supplement and with whom will they cooperate are extremely practical questions
which they must face, and also width the col- leges and schools must face. Giving
help to my competitor is in a sense the equivalent of doing harm to me. This was
precisely the point of danger.

THE STATED PURPOSES OF THESE FOUNDATION'S.

First, then, what are the aims of these foundations, and what limitations are placed
upon the funds which they are to manage? For these we must turn to their founding
documents.

1. THE PEABODY EDUCATION FUND.

The Peabody Education Fund, the gift of George Peabody, of Massachusetts, was
established in 1S07, and amounted finally to 3,000,000. In a letter to 15 men whom
be had chosen to act as his trustees, Mr. Peabody Bets forth his plans and purposes,
which were later embodied in the act of incorporation. He says:' I jrive to you the sum
of one million dollars, to be by you and your successors hold in trust, and the income
thereof used and applied, in your discretion, for the promotion and encouragement
of Intellectual, moral, or industrial education among the young of the more destitute
portions of the Southern and Southwestern States of our Union, my purpose being that
the benefits Intended shall be distributed among the entire population, without other
distinction than their needs and the opportunities of usefulness to them.

in the following paragraph he empowers them to use 40 per cent of the principal
sum within the next two years, then adds another million to the gift, grants the trustees
power to incorporate, and further says: In case two-thirds of the trustees shall at any
time, after the lapse of 30 ars, deem it expedient to close this trust, and of the funds
which at thai time shall! In the hands f yourselves and your successors to distribute
aol less than twO-tbjrds among such educational and literary institutions, or for such
educational purposes as they may determine, in the- States foX Whose hen.-tit the
income is mw appointed to be used. The remainder t,, be distributed by the trustees
for educational or literary purposes wherever they maj deem it expedient.

This letter, together with a later one in which he says, "1 leave all the details of
management to then- (the trustees') own discretion." were embodied in the preamble
to the charter later issued by the state of New fork.

In June. ISO!), Mr. Peabody addressed to the hoard a letter of appreciation for
their sei i, e in Carrying out hi trust, in which he conveyed a i ift Of iritie. s worth
nearly a million and a half dollars. 1

These letters certainly stand oul as among the most remarkable documents in the
history of educational philanthropy to this time. There were only the mosl general

restrictions on the funds, and these were to end after 80 yean, leaving the trustees almosl entirelj free to dispose of the entire fund. The prool Of their great distinction. BS we shall see. lies in the fact that they have been the precedenl for uii similar subsequent foundations.

2. TJIK JOHN t SLATES 1 I

The BecOnd of these foundations was the John l Slater Fund tor the BduCS- tion of Preedmen, established on March. 1882, by i gift of si. ihhi. imhi i,, letter of date March 4, 1882 Mr. Slater Invites 10 men to form s corporation lor the admin D 01 the fund, and iii this letter he sets forth the pur poses be wishes to achieve, together with the r trlctions be places upon the gift He Dames ns the general object

Nor ProC Of 1 'unit. Vm I.;, Iff.

Pcajridj Bdoc i uini. it—. Pol ii. p, ii: jcr.

the uplifting of the lately emancipated population of the Southern States, and their posterity, by conferring on them the blessings of Christian education.

He seeks not only for their own sake, but also for the safety of our common country to provide them with the means of such education as shall tend to make them good men and good citizens education in which the instruction of the mind in the common branches of secular learning shall be associated with training in just notions of duty toward God and man, in the light of the Holy Scriptures.

The means to be used, he says, "I leave to the discretion of the corporation." He then suggests " the training of teachers from among the people " and " the encouragement of such institutions as are most effectually useful in promoting this training of teachers." Further on he adds: I purposely leave to the corporation the largest liberty of making such changes in the methods of applying the income of the fund as shall seem from time to time best adapted to accomplish the general object herein named.

He then, obviously drawing upon English experience, warns them against the possible evils of such endowments, and states that after 33 years they are to be free to dispose of the capital of the fund to the establishment of foundations subsidiary to these already existing institutions of higher education, in such wise as to make the educational advantages of such institutions more freely accessible to poor students of the colored race.

Finally, he urges the avoidance of any partisan, sectional, or sectarian bias in the use of the gift, and closes with reference to the success of the Peabody Education Fund as having encouraged him to establish this foundation. 3

This letter was embodied in the charter issued by New York State in April, 1882. In all the fundamentals these documents are a fair copy of the charter and instruments of gift in the case of the Peabody Education Fund.

3. THE CARNEGIE INSTITUTION.

The third of these foundations to take form was the Carnegie Institution of Washington. The trust deed by which it was established is of date January 28, 1902, and transfers to the trustees securities worth 10,000,000. (This sum has since been more than doubled.) In this instrument of gift Mr. Carnegie declares it to be his purpose to found in Washington an institation which, with the corporation of other institutions shall in the broadest and most liberal manner encourage investigation, research, and discovery show the application of knowledge to the improvement of mankind, provide such buildings, laboratories, books, and apparatus as may be needed; and afford instruction of an advanced character to students properly qualified to profit thereby.

It aims, he says: 1. To promote original research.

2. To discover the exceptional man in every department of study and enable him to make the work for which he seems specially designed his life work.

3. To increase facilities for higher education.

4. To increase the efficiency of the universities and other institutions of learning both by adding to their facilities and by aiding teachers in experimental studies.

5. To enable such students as may find Washington the best point for their special studies to enjoy the advantages of the museums and other numerous institutions.

8 For a copy of this letter and the charter see Proceedings of the John F. Slater Fund for the Education of Freedmen, 1883, p. 21 B.

See Carnegie Institution of Washington, Tear Book No. 1, 1902.

6. To insure the prompt publication and distribution of the results of scientific investigation.

Finally:

The trustees shall have power, by a majority of two-thirds of their number, to modify the conditions and regulations under which the funds may be dispensed, so as to secure thai these shall always be applied In the manner best adapted to the advanced conditions of the times; provided always thai any modifications shall be in accordance with tbe purposes of the donor, as expressed in the trust.

4. Mil GENERAL KDUCATION BOARD.

Following this in 100:5 the General Education Board was established by John D. Rockefeller. His preliminary gift in 1902 of 1,000,000 was followed in 190", by a gifl of 10,000,000, and this by a third gift f 32,000,000 in 1007. and a fourth, of sio.000.000, in 1909.

In the act of incorporation Mr. Rockefeller states the purposes of the foundation as follows:

Sec. 2. That the object of the said corporation shall be the promotion of education within the Onited states of America, without distinction of race, sex, or creed.

SEC."'. That for the promotion of SUCh object the said corporation shall have power to build. Improve, enlarge, or equip, or to aid others to build. Improve, enlarge, or equip, buildings for elementary or primary schools, industrial schools, technical schools, norma schools, training schools for teachers, or schools of any grade, or for higher institutions of learning or, in connection therewith, libraries, workshops, gardens, kite-hens, or other educational ac-to establish, maintain, or endow, or aid others to establish, maintain, or endow, elementary or primary schools, Industrial Bchools, technical schools, normal schools, training schools for teachers, or schools of anj grade, or higher institutions of learning; to employ or aid others to employ teach and lecturers; to aid, cooperate with, or endow associations or other corporations engaged In educational work within the United states of America, or i" donate to any such association or corporation any property or moneys which shall at any time be held by the said corporation hereby Constituted; to collect educational statistics and Information, and to publish and distribute documents ami reports containing the same, and In general to do and perform all things necessary or convenient for the promotion of the objecl of the corporation.

in a letter from John D. Rockefeller, r., of date March-. 1902, the con ditions which are to control the to which the money ma. be nt arc gel forth. These limitations were subsequently changed. Originally, however, referring to the above Btatemeni of purpose, the letter Bays:'

Dpon this understanding ray father hereby pledges to the board the sum of one million dollars (1,000,000) to be expended al Tetlon during s period

Of 10 years, and will make payments under such pledges from time to time requested by the board or it execute mmlttee through its duly author offlci

The second glfl is announced in a letter from lit V T. Gates, which siates the following coin'

The principal to be held in perpetuity as a foundation for education, the in come above expenses of administration to be distributed to. or used for the benefit of, such n titutlom of learning, at Bucb tune-, in such amounts, for such purpo i under such cond or employed in uqh other ways, as the board mav deem he t adapted i" promote a comprehensive system of higher oin at ion in 11,, Dnlted

The third glfl ted through a letter from Mr. Rockefeller, jr. ami the conditions controlling the f the money art

Deral Education i. at or It Activity. 1902 L914,. 212 ir.

ibi. l. p 218.

One-third to be added to the permanent endowment of the board, two-thirds to be applied to such specific objects within the corporate purposes of the board as either he or I may from time to time direct, any remainder, not so designated at the death of the survivor, to be added to the permanent endowment of the board.

Concerning the fourth gift Mr. Rockefeller says, through a letter from his son addressed to the board, that the gift is to be added to the permanent endowment of the board. Then follow these qualifications:

He, however, authorizes and empowers you and your successors, whenever in your discretion it shall seem wise, to distribute the principal or any part thereof, provided the same shall be authorized by a resolution passed by the affirmative vote of two-thirds of all those who shall at the time be members of your board at a special meeting held on not less than 30 days' notice given in writing, which shall state that the meeting is called for the purpose of considering a resolution to authorize the distribution of the whole or some part of the principal of said fund. Upon the adoption of such resolution in the manner above described, you and your successors shall be and are hereby released from the obligation thereafter to hold in perpetuity or as endowment such portion of the principal of such fund as may have been authorized to be distributed by such resolution.

This would seem to give the board very wide powers and to leave to the donor very little control aside from a part of the third gift specially reserved. Yet Mr. Rockefeller seems not to have been fully satisfied, for on June 29, 1909, he addressed a letter to the board saying:

Gentlemen: I have heretofore from time to time given to your board certain property, the principal of which was to be held in perpetuity, or as endowment. I now authorize and empower you and your successors, whenever in your discretion it shall seem wise, to distribute the principal or any part thereof, provided the same shall be authorized by a resolution passed by the affirmative vote of two-thirds of all those who shall at the time be members of your board, at a special meeting held on not less than 30 days' notice given in writing, which shall s, tate that the meeting is called for the purpose of considering a resolution to authorize the distribution of the whole, or some part of the principal of said funds. Upon the adoption of such resolution in the manner above prescribed, you and your successors shall be, and are hereby, released from the obligation thereafter to hold in perpetuity or as endowment such portion of the principal of such funds as may have been authorized to be distributed by such resolution.

It would be hard to think of a point at which this board could be given wider freedom in the exercise of its jurisdiction over these funds than is here granted by the founder.

5. THE CARNEGre FOUNDATION.

The fifth of these foundations, the Carnegie Foundation for the Advancement of Teaching, had its origin in a letter, of date April 16. 1905, in which Mr. Carnegie set forth to a group of 25 men whom he had chosen to act as his trustees the plan of his foundation. 7 In all he has placed 16,250,000 in the hands of this board. The plan is clearly stated in the charter which was obtained in March, 1906. Here the object is declared to be:

To provide retiring pensions, without regard to race, sex, creed, or color, for the teachers of universities, colleges, and technical schools in the United States, the Dominion of Canada, and Newfoundland, who, by reason of long and meritorious service, or by reason of old age, disability, or other sufficient reason, shall be deemed entitled to the assistance and aid of this corporation, on such terms and conditions, however, as such corporation may from time to time approve and adopt.

1 Quoted in full in the first annual report of the president and treasurer of the Carnegie Foundation for the Advancement of Teaching.

Then follows the limitation that those connected with any institution which is controlled by a seel or which Imposes any theological test as a condition of entrance Into r connection therewith are excluded.

in general, to do and perform all things necessary to encourage, uphold, and dignify the profession of the teacher and the cause of higher education, and to promote the object of the foundation, with full power, however, to the trustee hereinafter appointed and their successors, from time to time to modify the conditions and regulations under which the work shad be carried on, so as to secure the application of the funds in the manner best adapted to the iditions of the times; and provided that by two-thirds vote the trustees may enlarge or vary the purposes herein set forth, provided that the objects of the corporation shall at all times he among the foregoing and kindred thereto."

6. THE RU88EIX SACK FOUNDATION.

In April, 1907, the sixth. if these, the Russel Sage Foundation, was chartered by the state of New York. The charter states the purpose of the corporation to be that of

Receiving and maintaining a fund or funds and applying the Income thereof to the improvement of social and living conditions In the United States of America, it shall be within the purposes of said corporation to use an means to that end which from time to time shall seem expedient to its members or trustees, including research, publication, education, the establishment and maintenance of charitable or benevolent activities and Institutions, and the aid of any such activities, agencies, or Institutions already established.

In her letter of gift, of date April 19, 11)07, Mrs. Sage says: " I do QOl wish to enlarge or limit the powers given to the foundation by its act of Incorpo ration," but adds that it seems wise to express certain desires t which ahe would wish the trustees to conform. Then follows several suggestions relative to local and national use of the funds, types of Investments, etc., which in ih writer's Judgment tend to enlarge the Freedom which most men serving as trustees would otherwise have been Inclined to exercise over the funds under the charter.

7. THh I'll 1.1 I'S SilikKS I I Mi.

The seventh of these foundations was the Phelps-Stokes Fund of nearly 1,000,000, which was established by the bequest of Caroline Phelps Stokes, who made her will in 1893 and died in 1909. The foundation was chartered in 1911. In leu- will Miss Stokes-ays: " I direct that all my residuary estate shall be given by my executors to the following persons" (here she name- the trustees sin- has chosen, and add

To Invesl and keep Invested bj them and their sui. the Interesl and net inc. mi. of such fund to be used by them and their successors for the erec-or Improvement of tenement bouse dwellings In New York Oitj for the poor families of New fork Cltj and for educational purposes Id the education of the both in Africa and the United States, North American Indians, ami needs and deserving white students through industrial schools of kln similar to that at Northfleld, Mass, In which Mr, Dwlght L, m Ij Is inter ted, or to the Peei industrial School at Ashevllle, n 0., the foundation of olarshlps and the erection or endowment of school bulldln. J hereby give said tru ad their successors full power of sale, public or private. In their discretion, upon such terms as they think b lectins any part of said trust fund in the course of the due execution of such trust,"

A.-t of lm Rulei for Granting of Retiring Allowance t," s v.

.- copiei,, r n. i of th. charter th in Indebted to Dr, John i

Qlenn, director of the. limitation.

i nun Pbelpa Btokas i unci Act of Incorporation, r. j Laws, and Othai Dot umenta,

The charter, in defining the purpose of the foundation, uses much of this same language and in addition the following: It shall be within the purpose of said corporation to use any means to such ends, including research, publication, the establishment and maintenance of charitable or benevolent activities, agencies, and institutions, and the aid of any such activities, agencies, or institutions already established. 11

This fund stands as a permanent endowment, but with such very general conditions placed upon its use that it is virtually as free as it could be made.

8. THE ROCKEFELLER FOUNDATION.

The latest foundation of just this type to be established is that of the Rockefeller Foundation, incorporated in April, 1913. The purpose of the corporation is that of receiving and maintaining a fund or funds, and applying the income and principal thereof, to promote the well-being of mankind throughout the world.

Its means are to be research, publication, the establishment and maintenance of charitable, benevolent, religious, missionary, and public educational activities, agencies, and institutions, and the aid of any such activities, agencies, and institutions already established, and any other means and agencies which from time to time shall seem expedient to its members or trustees."

9. THE CLEVELAND FOUNDATION.

There is one other type of foundation that is of very recent origin, but which is rapidly becoming popular, and shows promise of becoming very extensive and powerful in the near future. The chief work of this corporation is not education, but since educational service is within its powers it deserves mention here. The Cleveland Foundation, organized in January. 1914, was the first of this type, since followed by the Chicago Community Trust, the Houston Foundation, the Los Angeles Community Foundation, the St. Louis Community Trust, the Spokane Foundation, and other foundations of similar character at Milwaukee, Boston, Indianapolis, Ind., Attleboro, Mass., Minneapolis, Detroit, and Seattle. The Cleveland Foundation was formed by resolution of the board of directors of the Cleveland Trust Co., in which the company agreed to act as trustee of property given and devised for charitable purposes, all property to be administered as a single trust. The income of this foundation is administered by a committee appointed partly by the trustee company and partly by the mayor, the judge of the probate court, and the Federal district judge. The principal is managed by the trustee company.

The resolution creating the trust sets forth the object of the foundation as follows:
u

From the time the donor or testator provides that income shall be available for use of such foundation, such income less proper charges and expenses shall be annually devoted perpetually to charitable purposes, unless principal is distributed as hereinafter provided. Without limiting in any way the charitable purposes for which such income may be used, it shall be available for assisting charitable and educational institutions, whether supported by private donations or public taxation, for promoting education, scientific research, for care of the sick, aged, or helpless, to improve living conditions, or to provide recreation for all classes, and for such other charitable purposes as will best make for the mental, moral, and physical improvement of the 11 Ibid., p. 5 ff.

12 An Act to Incorporate The Rockefeller Foundation, in Ann. Rep.

8 From "The Cleveland Foundation a Community Trust," The Cleveland Trust Co., 1914.

Inhabitants of the city of Cleveland, as now or hereafter constituted, regard-of race, color, or creed, according to the discretion of a majority in number of a committee to be constituted as hereinafter provided.

It is further provided that if contributors to the foundation, in their instruments of gift, place limitations as to the final disposition of the principal, or as to the uses tn which its income may be put, or as to whal members of the trust company shall exercise control over the disposition of principal or Interest, then

The trustee shall respect and be governed by the wishes as so expressed, but only in so far as the purposes Indicated shall serin to the trustee, under conditions as they may hereafter exist, wise and most widely beneficial, absolute discretion being vested in a majority of the then members of the board of directors of the Cleveland Trust Go. to determine with reaped thereto.

When by the exercise of this power funds are diverted from the purposes indicated by their respective donors, such finals "shall be used and distributed for the general purposes of the foundation."

The foundation is to provide a committee for distributing its funds, the committee to be made up of

Residents of Cleveland, men or women Interested in welfare work, poe big a knowledge of the chic, educational, physical, and moral needs of the community, preferably but one. and In no event to exceed two members of said committee to belong to the same religious seel or denomination, those holding or seeking political office to be disqualified from serving.

Two members of the committee are to be appointed by the Cleveland Trust Co., one by the mayor, one by the senior or presiding judge of the conn which settles estates In Cuyahoga County, and one by the senior or presiding judge of the United states District Court for the Northern Distrlcl of Ohio. This committee is t be provided with a paid secretary, but otherwise to receive expenses only.

There are other Interesting feature-, of this resolution, For Instance, when the income of any trust is available for use by the foundation

All or any portion of the property belonging to such trust may he listed for taxation, regardless of any statute exempting all or any part thereof by reason uf its applical to charitable purposes, if a majority of the heard of directors of the Cleveland Trust Co. shall so direct

And mere Important still is the provision that with the approval of two-thirds "f the entire board "f directors of the Cleveland Trust ',., given-it a meeting called specifically for that purpose, ail ,,! any part of the principal constituting the truBl estate may he used tor any purpose within the Bcope of the foundation, which maj have the approval of four members of said committee, providing that not to exceed 20 per cent of the entire amount held as principal shall he rsed during a period live. I V ears.

Careful provision is made for an annual audit Of all: OUnts, and full

Control of funds and properties is rested in the trustees Of the foundation.

This i-; clearlj a new method f handling philanthropy In a i it i an ordinary commission business with unusually g i Becuritj for its patrons, n the tandpolnl of the bank it promises fair though net lucrative profit it i- bo designed ai to keep Its but icluslvely for the city of Cleveland, that fortunes accumulated there by the few eventually may he turned back te the community in the form of some I public I ed at from another angle, it is a real community enterprise which ought to develop civic pride as well at contribute to the solution of to iclal and educational problems, it philanthropy possible for mall as well as large fortunes, and so tends to popularize giving. The large fund that promises to accumulate is always adaptable to whatever changes the future may bring. It is undoubtedly an interesting and important business and social experiment by which education may hope to profit.

This places before us in fairly complete form the aims and purposes of this rather new type of educational enterprise. The Anna T. Jeanes Foundation is very similar in character but deals with elementary education exclusively. Similarly there are numerous other foundations engaged in charitable, library, or research work whose founding instruments embody the same fundamental principles common to those here quoted and, viewed from the standpoint of the evolution of a theory of endowments, belong in the same class.

To state these principles in brief we may say, first of all, that the " purpose " is in every ease set forth in the most general terms and in brief and simple language; second, that the means for carrying out this purpose is left almost entirely to the trustees of the foundation; third, that the means, and to an extent in some cases even the purpose, is modifiable at the will of the trustees; and fourth, that there is no sectional, racial, denominational, political, or ecclesiastical control. In most cases the capital fund is to remain permanently intact, but in some cases the entire income and capital may be used and the trust terminated. The Peabody Education Fund illustrates how this latter plan has already operated in full. The possible scope of activities is practically national for all, and international for some, the boards of trustees are self-perpetuating, and they receive no pay for their services.

This means that there is every possibility for keeping these large sums of money, now amounting to more than 300,000,000, constantly in touch with the real educational needs of the country, and in these charters there seems no possibility that it will ever be necessary for any one of these foundations to continue to do any particular thing in any particular way as, for instance, to maintain " enough faggots to burn a heretic " in order to control the available funds to some entirely desirable and profitable end.

THE OPERATIONS OF THESE FOUNDATIONS.

The real test of these liberal provisions could come only when educational philanthropy as a business began actually to cope with the educational, social, and economic forces in the midst of which it sought a place of responsibility.

A half century of activity has passed since the first of these foundations began its work. During the first 15 years of this period the Peabody Fund stood alone. Then came the Slater Fund, after which 20 years passed before the next, the Carnegie Institution at Washington, was established. This foundation by Mr. Carnegie seemed to initiate a new era in respect both to the number and size of these endowments.

1. THE PEABODY EDUCATION FUND.

When the Peabody Education Fund began its work there were few public-school systems of consequence in the South, either city or State. With this fund Dr. Barnas Sears attacked this problem directly, and by 1875 had so popularized the idea that cities and States were taking over the schools which the fund had established. The next move was for the training of teachers for these schools. Arrangements were made to turn the University of Nashville to this purpose, its new name to be Peabody Normal College. This was done in 1875, and a large number of scholarships were established. Later, attention was turned to summer normals, to teachers' institutes, and gradually to the development of normal schools in each of the States.

Doctor Curry, who succeeded Doctor Sears, carried forward the development of normal schools, but in his work befjan to condition his gifts upon the State's making appropriations to go with them. Doctor Curry was repeatedly before State legislatures, defending the claims of public education; and when, in 1898, it was proposed to make final division of the fund by endowing one or more institutions, practically every

Southern State protested against it. This disposition of the fund was finally made in 1913-14, with the endowment of the George Peabody College for Teachers.

During the years 1868 to 1914 the foundation gave away 3,650,-556 to the following: 1. City public schools 1,148, 183 2. Normal schools 122 3. Teachers' Institutes 382, 755 4. George Peabody College 381 5. Scholarships 580, 665 6. Kducational journals 8,300 7. Summer schools 32,."00 8. Rural public schools "7. 800 9. State supervision of rural schools 77, 950 1" Educational campaigns 18, 500 11. County supervision of teaching 15,000 12. Miscellaneous 44,400

The final distribution of the fund, with its accrued income, was as follows:

George Peabody College for Teachers 1,."inn. Don

University of Virginia 40,000

University of North Carolina in, ooo

University of Georgia 40."

University of Alabama 40. OOO

University of Florida 10, '

University i ilppi 40.

Louisiana State University 40, ooo 1 aivi rslty of Arkansas 10, 000

University of Kentucky 40

Johns Hopkins University 6,000

University of South Carolina D00

University of Missouri Q I 1 Diversity of Texas 8,

Winihrop Normal 'olli-."-

John f. Slater Fund (education of negroes), estimated at 000

Table 86 win give Bome sllghl notion of the service rendered by the fund, if we keep In mind, iir-t. that d of the 11 States receiving nid from the fund in 1871 was Itself contributing a much as 800,000 for common schools, and thai ai least- of these States spenl less than 200,000 each; 4 and second, tiiat these-inns were so placed by the foundation aa to stimulate Interest In 1 he Idea of public Bchools. The difficulty of the t. isk which this foundation has performed mus1 nol be erlooked. it la specially noteworthy thai bono the beginning us agents worked In the open, franklj a propaganda enterprise. Both by addresses and by publications tin- people were kepi Informed as to Insl what the founds 1 Ion ouch I to '1".

Peabody 1 I I, Vol. VI, p. 1

Sep of 1. s. Commit oj

Table 36. Distribution of the pi fix of the Peabody Education Fund, 1868-19W, in 9 to 12 Southern State. 1

Dates.

States.

1868 35,400 1869 90,000 1870 90,500 1871 1 100,000 1872. 1873. 1S74. 1875. 1876. 1877. 1878. 1879. 1880. 1881. 1882. 1883. 1884. 1 ss5. 1886. 1887. 1888. 1889.

130,000 136,850 134,600 98,000 73,300 7 850 57,600 64,500 42,900 34,125 49,350 46,925 31,600 31,995 46,000 31,600 23,600 39,750

To Normal College, Nashville.

Scholarships in Normal College, Nashville.

3,000 3,000 15,000 5,000 11,000 13.000 4,000 8,000 9,500 9,900 10,100 10,000 10,500 7,800 10,950 1,900 1,900 12,300 10,400 25,975 16,150 20,700 21,200 20,970 IS,.500 24,300 17,800 26,4-50

Total grants.

35,400 90,000 90,.500 100,000 130,000 136,850 134,600 101,000 76,300 95,750 64,.500 87,800 66,350 64,100 73,509 77,125 62,700 63,065 66,400 49,200 77,150

Dates.

1890. 1891. 1892. 1893. 1894. 1895. 1896. 1897. 189S. 1899. 1900. 1901. 1902. 1903. 1904. 1905. 1906. 1907. 1908. 1909. 1910.

To States.

43,376 49,524 54, 800 47,500 39,688 34,551 49,019 45,100 45,700 45,114 43,604 41,300 41,100 36,673 38,400 52,500 54,500 35,000

Normal College,

Nashville.

28,250 14,350 14,000 13,200 11,600 20,300 6,212 9,900 14,600 14,750 15,100 14.600 14,600 14,600 16,600 25,500 37,500 45,000

Scholarships in Normal College, Nashville.

21,474 23,726 23.600 26,450 25,188 35.131 19,008 23,567 24,498 24,709 25,351 24,329 24,180 24,127 25,000

Total grants.

93,100 92,400 87,150 76,3 s 89.981 74,239 60,.567 84.79S 84,573 84,055 80,229 79,880 75,400 80,000 78,000 92,000 80,000 80,000 69,000 36,500 1 Compiled from Rept. of U. S. Commis. Educ. for 1903 and from An. Proc. of Peabody Educ. Fund.

It is easy to imagine that society might have been much more skeptical of such an agency than it seems to have been. The growth of public-school sys-tems and of normal and industrial schools in the South is evidence enough that the fund has been greatly useful, and its success stands as a monument to the capacity of the southern people to furnish the type of public opinion necessary to direct such a philanthropic force into useful channels. In this, however, public opinion would have failed had not its founder left it free to meet the changing conditions which came with the passing years. This, as our first exper'ment. must be pronounced a decided success and it must stand as an excellent precedent both for the future public and for the future philanthropist.

2. THE JOHN F. SLATER FUND.

The John F. Slater Fund was handled on so nearly the same lines, to so nearly the same ends, in the same territory, and for many years by the same agent as was the Peabody Education Fund that detailed examination of its work would add little if anything new to this discussion.

3. THE CARNEGIE INSTITUTION OF WASHINGTON, P. C.

The work of the Carnegie Institution of Washington is difficult to describe in terms that will show what its contribution has really been. 15 Tn explaining the policy for the future, it is made clear that " grounds already occupied will be avoided," 1 ' and that the institution considers that systematic education in universities, colleges, professional schools, and schools of technology, and the assistance of meritorious students in the early stages of their studies are already provided for and are therefore outside the scope of the foundation.

15 For brief description and historical development of the institution, see The Carnegie Institution of Washington Scope and Organization, Fourth issue, Feb. 4, 1915, bj the institution; also Seven Great Foundations, by Leonard I Ayrcs; also retrospective review of, in the Eleventh Year Book of the Institution.

10 Carnegie Institution of Washington, Year Book, No. 1, 1902, p. xli.

From the outset the institution has directed its work along four lines as follows: Large research projects covering a series of years and managed by; i corps of investigators; small research projects, usually directed by Bingle individuals and for a brief period; tentative Investigations h young men or women of aptitude for research; and publication of the results of its own Studies and Of meritorious work which would im it otherwise he readily published. The order of development ol its larger departments of research is worthy of notice here. The were as follows:

Department of Experimental Evolution D ber, 1903
Department of Marine Biology December, 1903
Department f Historical Research i' ember, 1903
Department of Economics and Sociology 11 January, 1904
Department "f Terrestrial Magnetism April. 1904
Solar Observatory December, 1904 graphical Laboratory December, 1005
Department of Botanical Research December, 1905
Nutrition Laboratory December, 1906
Department of Meridian Astronomy March, 1907
Department of Embryology December, 1914

To these larger fields of operation must be added special researches In almost every possible field, and even a easual reading f the annual reports of Hi" institution shows that the division of administration has Itself served as a research laboratory of no mean proportions."

From the nature of its work it is evident that the relations of the Institu-t "ii to universities and to learned societies would have to be guarded, This the institution has tried to do by keeping out of occupied fields and by deal ing with Individuals concerned with specific pieces of research. The outside world bas apparently raised little question as to the privileges and responsi bilities of this institution, i, ui with the society of scholars ii has numerous conflicts, if the brief hints in the reports of the president are Indicative of the content of his letter hies."" it is in the face of this type of public opinion that this institution win continue to adjust Itself t" its proper place in so ety, and also to work OUt a fundamental theory of administration for this new type of educational enterprise, which, together with its help in popular izing scientific method ami the use of the results of research, win constitute no small part of its total conl r lull ion.

Any study of the finances, or of the amount of work done, or of the number of studies published, or of the number of houses, laboratories, observatories, and '-hip-owned and utilized by the institution can add hut little to anj attempt to evaluate this type of philanthropic enterprise. The following table the annual appropriations and the TOlome and page extent of it- published researches is of some value, however, when we consider that tic sum- have been spent in fields that could not have been so fully explored If the serai hundred lnv Drs employed had been compelled to meet the ide upon the I me of a university professor: it i, i Hon In 1016 11 lbs president's stud "f definitions of "humanities" in the ttitti "i l'ii;; .1,1) the 14th Yi Itul Ion,

Table 37. Distribution of appropriations made by the Carneaie Institution of Washington, li)02-ivn. 1 1 From 16th Yearbook, p. 29. Cents omitted.

Several points about these figures are of interest. During the 16 years recorded id the table the unused funds have accumulated, furnishing a substantial reserve fund for special needs. Aside from the first three years from 45 to 60 per cent of the appropriations have been for large department project s; from 5 to 12 per cent have been for the smaller investigations, the tendency being to give rather less to this item; from 2 to 10 per cent have been for publications, also with a tendency to decrease. During the first year only a small appropriation was made, approximately S6 per cent of all going for administration. During the second year only about 15 per cent went for administration, and for the remaining years the amount has been 7 per cent or less, declining to only 3 or 4 per cent in the six years ending in 1917.

There are no figures with which these properly can be compared, but they stand as the experience of 16 years spent in developing an entirely new type of institution. To the universities of the country it has not only furnished a great stimulus to research, but it has also given much direct assistance by financing important pieces of investigation and by publishing finished pieces of research.

4. THE GENERAL EDUCATION BOAKD.

Mr. Rockefeller referred to the General Education Board as "an organization formed for the purpose of working out. ill an orderly and rut her scientific way, the problem of helping to stimulate and improve education in all parts of the country." 20

The experience of the Peabody Fund in cooperating with State, county, and city officials was at hand and had been thoroughly studied." Just how to cooperate with other forces, public and private, was the first specific problem of the General Education Board.

Rockefeller, John D. The Benevolent Trust, the Cooperative Principle in Giving. The Worlds Work, vol. 17, Jan. 1909.

Leaving aside the question of how this was accomplished in the matter of farm demonstration work and in elementary and secondary education in the South, we are concerned here with the board's work in the held of higher education.

n.- of the tonus of Mr. Rockefeller's second j ift to the hoard was thai stance should be given to such institutions of learning as the hoard may deem host adapted to promote a comprehensive system of higher education in the United States.

The fad was we had no system of higher education, and this corporative proposed to do what it could toward that most laudable end. Schools had horn developed by the church, the state, and private enterprise, each working with but little reference to the other, denominational competition and politics often resulting in quite the opposite of system.

If this new hoard w-as to work toward a "system of higher education," then ii must inevitably clash with these already conflicting enterprises, or somehow t a coordination of their various forces. Some definite DOUcy, therefore, had to be decided upon. Two principles Of procedure were laid down, as follows: The board neither possessed nor desired any authority, and would not seel; directly or Indirectly to bias the action of any college or university: in making an appropriation the board would in no way interfere with the Internal management of an institution nor incur any responsibility for its conduct.

When and where and how to apply these principles was the practical task. In HMO 17 the hoard reported thai In all it had assisted 112 colleges and universities in 32 Slides. During the year 1916 it the board contributed a total of 1,185,000 toward a total of 5,300,000 in gifts to 9 colleges. When we consider thai for this same year Harvard received from gifts as much as 1,934,947, Columbia 1,390,594, and Chicago 3,181,543 we can see thai the board had to find some basis for making choice among its many possible beneficiaries.

Making this choice was precisely what Mr. Rockefeller wanted to have done entifically. To do it was to demonstrate thai philanthropy could be made a successful business enterprise. Accordingly, extensive studies of the ques tion were undertaken, and to date almosl the entire college field has been surveyed with respect to certain main issues, and thorn lieges to which contributions ha e been made have been studied minutely. The result Is a mine of important and systematically organized Information aboul our higher In tutlons of learning thai had not hitherto been available These studies can nol be adequately described, nor their value satisfactorily explained in few

WOnlfl a method of giving thej stand as a permanent contribution Of value. They have meant that fact rather than sentiment ha guided the board from I"- start

The hoard has 11s: ii. a souiewhal modest statement " of certain clearly evident improvements that have resulted from then stiicl adherence to tins method- follow

First, is thai of more careful accounting systems,

Second, it has ne. d a clarification (certain terms, such as capital," "endowment," "scientific equipment," etc, the verj loose usage of which had r plenty "ii (lie in tl Uuil duuij benefi ii. General Education Board, 1902 1014, p 148 fr.

previously made it impossible to compare financial statistics of different institutions.

Third, it has put an end to the practice, rather common among colleges, of asing the principal of endowment funds on the assumption that the sum so taken was a loan and would later be replaced.

Fourth, it has brought about a distinction in practice between the educational budget of a college and its various business activities, such as the running of a boarding hall.

Fifth, it has resulted in a sort of departmental accounting, which has helped not only to distinguish costs in college from costs in preparatory departments but has tended to help even in defining what work is of college and what is of academy grade.

This board has operated on one other principle that deserves mention, viz, that any college that can not raise some money from its own natural clientele is scarcely to be thought of as very necessary to the community. Accordingly, it has been the practice of the board to contribute a sum toward a much larger total which the college must raise. Mr. Rockefeller said that to give to institutions th. it ought to be supported by others is not the best philanthropy. Such giving only serves to dry up the natural springs of charity. 24

The application of this principle has not only brought large gifts to education that probably would never have been given otherwise, but it has helped toward placing the responsibility for the growth of these colleges where it belongs upon large numbers of interested friends.

Another condition from which the board varies but rarely is that the entire gift, of which their own forms a part, shall be preserved inviolate for the permanent endowment of the institution. This recognizes the need for general, as opposed to special, endowment funds. Another provision is that no part of the board's gift can ever'be used for theological instruction.

During the last few years the board has entered upon two other lines of work that of financing and directing educational investigations and that of putting clinical instruction in the medical schools of John Hopkins, Yale, and Washington Universities upon a full-time basis. This latter was not an untried experiment, but it was certainly in an early experimental stage in this country.

The field of educational investigation was not new, but the demand for such work was by no means fully met by other agencies. The survey of the Maryland State school system; the more recent report of a survey of the schools of Gary, Ind.; and the experimental work on reading and writing scales at Chicago University and with gifted pupils at Illinois University: ms well as the experimental school at Teachers College. Columbia University. are suine of the results so far obtained in this field, all of which give large promise.

The following table will give at most an inadequate notion of the work that has thus far been accomplished by the foundation:

M In World's Work, above cited.

PHILANTHROPY IX MKRIOAX IMOHl. i: EDUCATION.

Tabu 38.-Total appropriations of the General Education Board from its foundation in 1H'i to June. V), 1918.

(The Rockefeller Fund

For negroes: (oueges iri'i ichools for current expenses and buildings,.

Medical schools for current expenses

Rural school agents

Summei nty train mi' jehools i tome-makers' Clubs

Expenses of special students at Hampton and Tusk'

Scholarships.

: iral School Fund

John F. Slater Fund

Agricultural work (white and negro

Sou' ' iltural demon; tr; Uion work.

Girls' canning and poultry work in the South i tin iral demon tratlon work ii imp hire agricultural demonstration work. Rural 716,077 .". bite an I tcatlonal In iron iti'inal conditions and net ountlne system fur G irj krd unmei i ii ' lei county organization i onfi ren i hind 1,440 716,077 113,751 7.772 11,000 Income on h tnd tune 30, 1918.

i a appropriated in I H u:. pt, I I'd. i 'i; 18, pp in addition t" the foregoing the sum of 110 ims been appropriated iin i paid t" negro rural achoola from the Income of inui t. Jeanea Fund, and 85,000 een appropriated and paid to Spelman Seminary fr the principal tie Laura 8 Rockefeller Fund.

HI FOUNDATION 1 OR I 1 I IOVANCEMRN1 01 mvim'.

Fundamental to Mr. Can of giving had been the idea that thi purpo for which 'iir glvea must nol bnve n degrading, pnuperl ndency upon the recipient. 11 To be able to L-i r. i pen Ion und avoid Buch 1111-111r aa thi Mr. '. gle el for himself r., i thai man evlla were resulting from low aalarlea for profewora and being familiar with the Idea "t teachers' penaiona- wldelj practiced In tta, p 21, fr.

Europe, Mr. Carnegie hoped to make the pension for the professor and his widow a regular part of the American educational system. He believed that if the teacher could receive his retiring allowance not as a charity but as a matter of right then pensions would raise the plane of academic life. 8

Obviously, the income from the original gift of, 10,000,000 would not meet tlie needs of the 700 or more institutions calling themselves colleges. First of all, therefore, the foundation was face to face with the question of what is a college. Secondly, having barred from participation in the fund all institutions under denominational control, the question of what constitutes denominational control must also be settled. The legal definition of a college which has Ijeeo iu operation in the State of New York furnished a basis for an answer to the first question, 27 and a definition of denominational college was arbitrarily decided upon and the foundation began operations, trusting to investigation and experience to clarify these definitions.

The first work of the foundation was to send out a circular asking all institutions of higher learning for information bearing upon: (a) The educational standards in use; (b) the relations of the school to the State, both in matters of control and support; (c) the relation of the school to religious denominations. In addition to this, information regarding salaries and size of faculties was asked for. 2 This brought together an unusually rich mass of educational data, which when digested by the foundation furnished the basis for its future action.

Out of this and succeeding studies came the quantitative definition of the college entrance " unit "; a clearer distinction between the work of a preparatory department and that of the college proper; as well as clearer conceptions of "college." of "State college," and of "denominational college." These accomplishments are pointed to here not only as an important contribution in standardization but also because of the wide discussion of these subjects which the action of the foundation provoked. Such work shows, top, how the foundation realized that in order to act wisely in the awarding of retiring allowances it must itself first of all become an "educational agency." 21 '

This type of study is not the extent of the foundation's educational investigations. Its charter demanded that the trustees "do and perform all things necessary to encourage, uphold, and dignify the profession of the teacher and the cause of higher education." 30 In pursuance of this end the foundation has from the start undertaken to contribute liberally to the scientific study of higher education. In 1913 Mr. Carnegie added 1,250,000 to the endowment to meet the needs of a research department, and already the results of 11 extensive studies have been published and several others are under way. It is not possible to state accurately the value of this type of contribution. One might point to specific cases of more accurate university bookkeeping having resulted from the issuance of Bulletin No. 3, 1910, which presented 25 typical blank forms for the public reporting of the financial receipts and expenditures of universities and colleges; or to the revision of standards and the stir that was caused in the medical world by the issuance of Bulletin No. 4, 1910, describing the status of medical education in the United States and Canada; or to the legislative enactments following the recommendations made in Bulletin No. 7, 1907, giv- 28 Sec The Policy of the Carnegie Foundation for the Advancement of Teaching, Educ Rev.,. Tune, 1006.

27 See First Annual Report of the President and of the Treasurer, p. 38.

Ibid., p. 10, ff.

-" See The Carnegie Foundation for the Advancement of Teaching. Second Annual Report of the President and Treasurer, p. 65.

80 Sec quotation on p. 85.

ing the results of the survey of education In the State of Vermont; r to similar reactions to tin reports dealing with engineering education and legal education, and In each Instance show that the stud; brought direct results. The larger value of such work, however, can not be measured In thai way.

The sentiment for better medical schools which was created by the foundation's study has been a powerful factor In bringing about higher standards of training in that profession, and similar valuable results hav me from other studies.

in administering the pension system the foundation has met with many difficulties, si. me of which have not been easy tn overcome. Prom the outset the foundation has wisely dealt with Institutions and UOt with individuals. It mihst not he said, however, that the foundation s,. itself up as a standarding agency. It did set itself up as an educational agency, and very properly Chose tn administer its funds in terms of educational standards of its own choosing. In doing this no embarrassment was felt. The foundation named a list of "accepted institutions," 31 explained why these were included, and in. MTiiius criticism of this list was offered by the public

By the end of the first year the trustees stated that the questions of educational standards and of denominational or State control had been provisionally dealt with." These questions continued to bring difficulties to the foundation, and for several years their reports show that they were exhaustively studied. The question of pensions for professors of State universities was solved in 1908 when Mr. Carnegie addressed a letter to the hoard in which he offered l' add 5,000,000 tn the endoWmenl in order to meet that need."

Denominational colleges memorialized the trustees ti modify their ruling af fecting such institutions' hid with little success. Several sharp criticisms of the position oi the foundation in this matter appeared in magazines, 11 hut the trustees preferred to maintain their original standard."

During the first few years the number of Institutions eligible for the "accepted list" Increased at an unexpected rate" and the foundation was com xlli (I to re is (. it rules for granting pensions or Otherwise plan to carry a heavier load. Within a very few years a number of colleges under denomtna tioiiai control, by proper legal process, had so modified their charters or articles of incorporation as to make them eligible t" the accepted list," th 'lginal nctuarlal figures had taken no account of the growth of the

Institutions," and the number retiring under the "years of service" basis bad been far greater than anticipated," ami othei facts Indicated that some modification of original

Phe original list u printed in tin foundation'! Aral annual report above. ii. it e the foundation'! i t annual report above cited, p 86 IT.-.- the foundation' third annual report, p 62, for copj of ill letter. " s-e the foundation'! fourth annua report, p i ft.

. icttei by J. P. published In Nation, '. i BO, p 288, and othei arrjeh li tin- hd(volume; also vol 81 of Science.

gle foundation tot the Ikdvanoement. f Teaching. Report, 1909, p

"Carnegie Foundation fei the Ad menl of Teaching Report, 1909, p

Bowdoin, Drury, Central Unlveraltj of Kentucky, and io. iw. Unlvei m are iiius

Sri the foundation! fourth annual report, p in in. Ravlea of Bis k eai of tdmlnletrative experience the prealdent of the founds tiou exp ' i. that the ' lie had been "adopted bj the Lru udei it.,. i mnption that but fea ap lid be made undei It and thai tbeae would n li.- main application! f n arho. i r. i furtbei aervlce The Inten iinn u. i in f. n i to uae the rule a a i on Lftei i fea yea ra of admin la (ration II perfi u that the i lie wa dolni harm rathei than good, ti m tiii i. i bj the ii nee with the aulhorltj the had I In tin-ii ii. iii. i-." and a llitj rule. Bei enth. ninii. ii report. f the , i. in and ii 1912, p 82.

plans would have to be made. At the outset the right to make such modification had been specially reserved," partly upon the advice of actuarial experts. Accordingly, in 1009 the rules for granting retiring allowances were changed in two respects.

The original rules based the grant of a pension upon age or length of service in accordance with 10 specific rules. Rule 1 was revised to include instructors as well as the various grades of professors, deans, and presidents, and so really broadened the scope of the foundation's work to that extent. The original rules granting a pension after 25 years of service were changed so as to restrict such allowance to only such teachers as were proved by medical examination to be unlit for service. This latter change brought forth extensive criticism, raising the question of the ethical right of the foundation to do the thing it had specifically reserved the right to do, viz, to modify its rules " in such manner as experience may indicate as desirable."

The reasons for making these changes are more fully set forth in their 1904 report than it is possible to show in brief space. It serves our purpose here to note, first, that such change was made, and that the foundation was legally within its rights in so doing; and, second, that the change met with strong opposition in many quarters.

There were slight modifications of these rules, but no important changes were proposed until the issuance to the trustees and to all teachers in associated institutions of the foundation's confidential communication in 1915, setting forth a Comprehensive Plan of Insurance and Annuities." This communication called attention to the weak points in the existing system of pensions and proposed to replace the old system with a plan of insurance and annuities. More than 50 institutions complied with the request for criticism, and their statements are published in an appendix to the eleventh annual report of the foundation. Many faculties approved the plan in part, a few approved the plan in lull as suggested, but altogether these statements, together with what appeared in the press, contain many important criticisms. It was argued, first, that the Carnegie Foundation had created certain expectations on the part of college teachers which it was morally obligated to fulfill; second, that it is unjust to establish a system of insurance involving compulsory cooperation on the part of every teacher; and, third, that commercial companies could offer o plan which would be financially more attractive."

In 1916-17 the trustees passed a resolution referring the proposed new plan of insurance and annuities to a commission consisting of six trustees of the foundation, two representatives of the American Association of University Professors, and one representative each from the Association of American Universities, the National Association of State Universities, and the Association Of American Colleges. 44 This commission agreed upon a plan of insurance ' See original Rules for Granting of Retiring Allowances in first annual report, -This was later published as Bulletin No. 9 of the foundation.

43 In the eleventh annual report of the president and treasurer President Tritchett virtually accepts the first of these objections as valid (see p. 24), and the trustees passed a resolution approving the idea of a contributory pension system which will operate " without unfairness to the just expectations of institutions or of individuals under the present rules." (See p. 4.) In the twelfth annual report a review of the year's work points out that the experience of 1'2 years' work has found the foundation " faced with two duties: First, to carry out fairly and to the best of their ability the obligations assumed in the associated institutions"; and, secondly, to establish a system of insurance. Further the report says: "In the nature of the ease the determination of what is a reasonable exercise of the iower of revision retained by the trustees tout lies many personal interests." See pp. If) and 30.

"Twelfth An. Rep. of the Foundation, 1!)1G-17, p. 5, for the membership of this commission.

and annuities and recommended it u the trustees of the foundation. 41 In May. 1917, it was voted to approve the fundamental principles of the teachers' pen-sii. n Bystem and also the combination of Insurance and annuity benefits as fined in tin-repori of the above commission

This very Boon led to the organization of the Teachers' Insurance and Annuity Association of America, chartered by the State of New Xork n March 4. mis. Tins Insurance company, together with a definite and fair plan for fulfilling the expectations of teachers who had belonged to the associated insti tutions under tin original pension system, brought u a close what Is likely in be regarded as the first period of the history of the Oai Foundal for the Advancement of Teaching, it was In many ways a stormy period in which sharp and often personal criticism was hurled at the foundation bj individual-, through the press and even in thp form of an Investigation by the Federal Commission on Industrial Relations. Few dired replies to these criticisms have been made by the officers of the foundati xcepl through tl pages of their regular annual reports, where every Intelligent criticism has been dealt with.

It is obvious, even Erom this brief Bketch of the history of this foundation, that what may he termed the elastic clause in its rules for granting pensions has been a most Important one. The field was new and experience alone could point the way. Without the right ti change its plans the foundation mighl have become a nuisance instead of a blessing. It thai clause has given Hip foundation an easy way out of difficulties tee easy a- Borne have thoughl it has proved to he an excellent point of leverage for public opinion, ami it must he evident to all that public opinion has not been Ignored.

It must he-: iii that the fountlatin has done Borne difficult pioneering in the field of teachers' pensions and has contributed liberally to the development ami application "i proper standard-, in the field of higher education. The follow tables will give. a partial financial i- the operations "t the foundation up to June SO, 1817:

Receipts and expenditures Camegu Foundation n Idvancenieni of Teaching, ."; ."'.."

fill 500, hi total.

i 731.413 : k to Part II, for a full i '-i"" of t: m. 18 a ni ii, ic b Pi f "i ""i dlgnlflrd replj t lucb for i ' 116, "Bbould the arnei i i a indatlon be Bun aod in nddr- i, f iii, ii,, t of Sup., Na(i d oc, In 1018 indatlon In mei. i Education Tbii ail

Table 40. Foundation's expenditures for allowances, each third year?

Years.

Institutions.

Kind.

I (Associated

Nonassoeiated.

ions o IAssociated.

Nonassociated.

Associated l Nonassociated.

i (Associated i Nonassociated.

'(Associated ; Nonassociated.

1906 2.

1911-12. 1914-15.1 191G-173

Number.

Retired teachers on roll.

Retiring allowances paid.

6,475 206,473 104,537 388,338 108,330 473,969 99,851 345,214 62,054

Widows' pensions.

Number.

Amount paid.

1,125 8,317 53,646 20,046 80,152 116,891 23,199

Total amount paid.

16,604 6,600 231,018 112, 853 441,985 128,438 554,122 120,603 462,105 85,253

! The amounts for the intervening years are not given, but approximate those here reported; see 12th An. Rep. of the foundation. Cents are omitted. 1 From July 1 to Sept. 30. Oct. 1 to June 30.

6. THE RUSSELL SAGE FOUNDATION.

The Russell Sage Foundation has purposely avoided the field of higher education from the start, 48 but deserves mention here because of the contributions it has made to educational research.

Among its contributions are to be listed studies of retardation and elimination in city school systems, the medical inspection of schools, the care and training of crippled children, child-welfare work, health work in public schools, education through recreation, school buildings and equipment, and many other studies of direct or indirect value in reducing education to a science. Important, too, is the extensive work which the foundation has done in the held of educational surveys. The reports of the Springfield and the Cleveland surveys have aided materially in the establishment of standards for this kind of work. From the start the foundation's policy has been to spend its income on research and the dissemination of knowledge with a preventive intent. That it lias carried out such a policy is evident to those who are familiar with its publications.

SUMMARY.

In this chapter it has been the purpose to describe the working principles and as far as possible to show the significance of our recently established philanthropic educational foundations. In form these foundations represent a new type of agency in educational philanthropy. In scope the possibility of service which they are empowered to render to higher education is almost without limit, and in the main each of the foundations occupies a field peculiarly its own.

These foundations are well characterized as attempts at reducing educational philanthropy to a business. The corporate principle is fully applied and the plan of administration is similar to that by which the affairs of a factory or a railroad are directed. In their most recent form the essential principles of a commission business are employed.

They are further characterized by the very genera) limitations placed upon the gifts by the founders; by the possibilities left open for reasonable changes in the original purpose, or even, in some cases, for a termination of the entire 48 Schneider, Franz, jr. The Russell Sage Foundation, in Jour. Nat. Institute of So. Sciences, Die. 20, 1915, p. 5.

trust; by the very eareful plans devised for the administration of tlie funds; and by the entire absence of political, sectarian, or Bectional control.

I be work accomplished iy these foundations can ut be fully evaluated. In variety and extent it Includes gifts and propaganda for the development of public schools, the endowment of colleges, fellowships, and pensions, as well as research In almost everj field known to science, in all these Belds their efforts have been fruitful.

The movement for in the history of educational philanthropy it must be called a distinct movement) apjh-ars not yet to have reached its zenith. In character it is becoming more ami more Inclusive, and perhaps by that tendency may contribute to the establishment of the idea thai education is but one of the many aspects of our social problem. The power which such institutions can turn toward the reconstruction of society has already been clearly indicated bj the results described above, but quite as clearly has public opinion shown not Only Its ability to discern the possible misuses Of that power but also its readiness to brim: pressure to bear once a i 'n of such danger has been sensed. Bowever much these foundations may supervise, therefore, and the promise in this respect is great, it is evident that they will themselves not go unsupervised.

Chapter VI.

SUMMARY AND CONCLUSIONS.

PURPOSE AND PLAN OF THE STUDY.

It has been the purpose of this study to inquire into the extent to which philanthropy has been responsible for the development of our institutions of higher learning, to discover what motives have prompted this philanthropy and how these motives have influenced college building, and, in addition, to try to bring to light whatever has been developed in the way of a theory of educational philanthropy and of educational endowments.

The study is covered in four chapters dealing, respectively, with: (1) The development of a theory of endowments and of philanthropy; (2) philanthropy of the colonial period; (3) philanthropy of the early national period, 1776-1865; (4) philanthropy of the late national period. 1865-1918; and (5) great educational foundations.

Various sources have been drawn upon, chief of which have been indicated by footnote references. These sources may be classified as having to do with what may be termed the qualitative and quantitative aspects of the problem, respectively. The former including charters, constitutions, by-laws, deeds of trust, wills, and other instruments of gift; the latter only with the bare figures and their analysis, or the statistics, of such gifts.

THE THEORY OF ENDOWMENTS.

At the beginning of college building in America there was no special theory of educational endowments or of educational philanthropy to work from. No careful thought had been given to the subject in England aside from discussions of practical situations, numbers of which were demanding attention long before America began to build colleges.

About the time Harvard College had reached its first centennial a really subsfnntial discussion of the subject was entered upon in Europe and has continued practically ever since. The discussion was in connection with the general inquiry into the social institutions of the times, and represents one line of inquiry pursued by the new school of political economy just then taking form. Turgot, of France; Adam Smith, of England; and William von Humboldt, of Germany, were the chief early contributors in their respective countries and agree fairly well that education should not be endowed by the State, but rather that it should take its place in competition with all other interests. Turgot and Smith would modify the application of this laissez faire principle to meet certain conditions, while Humboldt would have it carried to its full length. Doctor Chalmers, curly In the nineteenth century, and John Stuart Mill, in 1833, however, proposed an important distinction between need for food and need for education, and urged that because of this difference the principle of free trade could not properly apply t education.

Owing Id the bad state of educational endowments In England; it that time, the discussion shifted somewhat to a consideration of the rights of the State in the control nt" endowments The critics declared that the failure of thi endowments was due to the very principles involved in endowments for education, while the Mill economists argued that it was due merelj ti failure of the State tn exercise a proper control over them.

Other discussions in England of the possible value of endowments followed, involving the question of the right of posthumous disposition of property and emphasizing the rights of society (the State) as the real recipient of such gifts

EARLY EXPERIENCES IN AMERK.

in the early years America contributed little to this theoretical discussion, hut as time went on and the idea of free public education began to take root. we gradually came face to face with it in connection with the question of school support. The State had taken a hand in initiating and in the support of our first attempt at higher education. The chinch had taken even a larger part than that shared by the state, in colonial Massachusetts, however, the

State and the church were practically one, and therefore no opposition!"

tween the two was likely to appear. The church and the state In America were soon to rest upon the theory of complete separation, however, and then the question of responsibility for the support of schools had to be worked out The boilding of colleges went on, the church, the state, and private philanthropy sharing the burden of cost, but with the responsibility for management resting mainly with the church until near the close of the colonial period.

At the beginning of the national period the state began to contribute less and less to the old foundations ami to debate the question of state colleges or universities, By the middle of the new centurj the movement for state support and control of higher education took definite form. This did not rule out the churdi "I- private philanthropy, nor did it consciously Interfere with them, it. nevertheless, set up competition between these two ideas of educational control. The result has been the development of a rather large literature on tin- Bubject, a decided stimulus to higher quality of work, and a clarification of the respective functions of the church ami the state in h gher education. in the earlier decades private philanthropy was so complete! dominuted bj the church on the one hand, and w. i v,,-mall and BCattered "ii the oilier, that it-place in tin- field of higher education had raised no serious questions development ol state universities, however, brought criticism, ami in more tich college buildings as that Initiated bj Ezra Cornell, Johns Hopkins, John D Rockefeller, Leland Stanford, and Andrew Carnegie, and such nunt;11 hlng foundation as those discussed In 'ha pier v have raised the question in- possible good or ill thai maj come from state endow mem and from private philanthropy on such a large scale it i- In connection with these two points in our educational experience the h between state and chun h control; and the upsetting of Id and small practice by wealthy philanthropists through the launch ng of great competing universities, or by the establishment ol vast fundi for endowment, pensions, and Investigation that America's contribution to a theorj of endowments or of educational phllanthropj has been mad'-. Writer-, on social and political theirs have given the subject but little thought, though man legislative bodies have dwelt at length upon specific issues which have been raised by the clash of these foives. 1 In colonial America the aim of higher education was from the start dominated by the general religious aim of the people, and whether the State and the church were one or not, it was almost without exception the church leaders who initiated the move for building a college, and the colleges of this period were primarily designed for the training of ministers.

The colonial governments of Massachusetts, Virginia, Connecticut, and New-York contributed liberally to the maintenance of Harvard, William and Mary, Yale, and King's Colleges, respectively, but not so with Rhode Island, New Jersey, and New

Hampshire in the case of Princeton. Brown, Dartmouth, and Rutgers. We are able to say, therefore, that philanthropy, motivated in the main by religion, was primarily responsible for initiating college building in all cases; that it was largely responsible for the maintenance of five of the nine colonial colleges, and almost solely so for the other four. We may say, too, that while the idea of State support for colleges was practiced, it was not common in all the Colonies, and in no case (William and Mary a possible exception) did a Colony assume full responsibility in the founding and development of a college. Hence denominational rather than State lines stand out in the history of higher learning in colonial times, and unless we think of the impetus given to " this worldly " education by Franklin in the beginnings of the University of Pennsylvania there was no experiment that could be called a real departure from the traditional idea of a college.

The sources from which philanthropy came during these years were numerous and varied, and each has in a way left its mark upon the college it benefited. No small amount of assistance came from England, largely through the influence of religious organizations. The influence of these gifts is suggested by the names of several of our colleges. Again, funds were sought in Ibis country in Colonies qhite remote from the college, and in many cases substantial aid was thus received. In the main, however, a college was either a local community or a denominational enterprise. If the former, as in case of Harvard, the burden rested mainly upon people close by. If the latter, as in the case of Brown, then churches of the denomination in question, wherever located, gave freely to its support. Many gifts from towns and from church congregations are also recorded.

One is impressed at every point with the very large number of small gifts and with the way in which they were obtained. This applies to the entire history of American college building. The thousands of small gifts to our colleges seem to record the fact that from the outset these were to be schools of the people.

During this period philanthropy initiated no unique educational experiments, yet it is quite as true to say that neither do we find evidence that gifts anywhere inlluenced education in a wrong way. Gifts which were made to some specific feature of a college went in the main to the library, to professorships, to scholarships, and to buildings, all of which are essential to any college. Throughout this period, however, it has been shown that a relatively large percentage of gifts were made to the college unconditionally.

We may say, then, that our beginnings were small; that they were warmly supported by the mother country; that the idea of State support was common, though by no means universal; that there is evidence that no State, with the possible partial exception noted, intended to assume full responsibility for the 1 Note, foi instance, tbe legislative debates in New York over the founding of Cornell I'liiversity.

college; thai philanthropy clearly iiii assume thai responsibility; and that philanthropy did direct the policy of every college We way say that philanthropy was motivated by religion, and that 11 church in must rases dominated the movement; thai penury was common in all cases: thai the thousands f small gifts constituted an Important asset in that they popularised the idea f the college and bo help d to democratize society: and thai the gifts were in the main " to the college" without condition, or. it' conditioned, they were almost invariably in accord with the essential lines of the school's growth,

THE EARLY NATIONAL PERIOD.

During the early national period there was no special break in the main forces that had been building colleges in the Colonies. Conditions under which these forces had to work, however, were vastly different, whether we think of the problems of state making, of religion, of industries, of exploration and settlement, of growth of population, or of social philosophy, it was an age of expansion in all these matters and that in a broad and deep sens '.

In the matter of higher education it was also an age of expansion; expansion in numbers of colleges, and. to some extent at least, in educational aim and types of si tidies offered.

The Revolution had brought to an end the work of English philanthropy. and in Increasing measure state support for established colleges was declining, leaving the task mainly to the chinches of the country. The question of tin-Stale's function in higher education was soon raised, however, and before the close of the period a solution of the theoretical aspect of the problem had been reached ami several state universities well established.

Whatever Of promise there was In this new movement, however, the great colic-,- pioneering of this period was done almost entirely h church-directed philanthropy.

In this period,: ts in colonial days, the beginnings were small. Academies were often established with the hope that in time they would become colleges, the financial penury so common to the early colleges was characteristic through- oul this period, and the subscription list was common everywhere

The motive behind the work of the church was not oiii to spread the Gospel hut to provide schools tor the training of ministers to mi the Increasing number of vacant pulpits reported throughout the period. Denominational lines were strong and undoubtedly led to an awkward distribution of collegi

The motive-, hack of philanthropy in this period differ little therefore from tiios,. common to early Harvard, rale, and Princeton. Among the older col le- 'es. win-re the curriculum had beguU to broaden and professional schools to ' in, it was somewhat more common to liinl gifts made to some par ticular end, A ng the newer Foundations we see a fair duplication of the earl history of the older colleges, except that the new colleges grew some what more rapidly. Then- is in most cases a more marked tendency to give toward permanent endowment, while among the conditional ifts those tor pro md out strongly everywhere, and litis to indigent students suffer a decline,

Tin- development of profe nlonal schools, of the manual labor college ami of Institutions for the higher education of women mark a change In our educational phllosophj ami give expression to the changing s, i,. i m,. of the time- Mosl of n. laments won- initiated ami fostered 03 philanthropy.

Medical and law school originated malnlj private schools conducted for profit, while schools "i theologj have been philanthropic enterprises from the Iff. The Idea of women's COllegcJ 111:1 ha e originated in the private pay schools for girls, or ladies' seminaries, common in the South, but the first well-fin;! need college for women was the work of philanthropy, as most all subsequent attempts have been, and description of the work of philanthropy in these schools would fit fairly well any college of the period.

The fact that we find philanthropy rising to meet these many and varied educational and social ideas and ideals is not only an important fact in the social life of this country but is also an important characteristic of our educational philanthropy.

It is early in this period that the church education society comes into existence to answer the call of the church for more and better trained ministers. The work of these societies was extensive, and no doubt resulted in filling many vacant pulpits and church missions.

During this period, then, we may say that philanthropy did not slacken its interest in higher education, either because of the loss of English support or because of the rise of the State university. Philanthropy was, as before, directed in the main by the churches, and so through the whole period is prompted in the main by religious motives. The church college followed the westward-moving frontier, leaving many evidences of denominational competition for the new field. The failure of these church schools to meet the demands of the ministry is marked by the rise of church education societies whose aim was to provide scholarships and loans for students who would enter the ministry. Philanthropy was active in the movement toward separate professional schools, in the development of manual labor colleges, and in the origin and development of women's colleges during this period. These new enterprises may with some propriety be called educational experiments, credit for which must go to churches and to philanthropy.

As to method, there is practically nothing new to record. Permanent endowment grows somewhat more popular, and gifts for specified purposes tend to replace gifts to the general'funds of the college. Nowhere, however, are the main aspects of the college neglected in favor of the new or unusual features.

THE LATE NATIONAL PERIOD.

After 1865 we enter a period of vast expansion in college building as in every other line. The idea of State higher education was worked out, and the question of State versus private and church schools was, for most people, satisfactorily solved. In the new States of the period it was more often the State than the church that established the pioneer institution for higher learning. With the exception of the manual labor college, practically all old ideas and practices in higher education were continued in force. Separate professional schools, women's colleges, church boards of education, and the typical small church college, all went forward, and each seems to have found a place for itself and still shows signs of healthful growth.

The period is equally well characterized by the development of new enterprises, back of which were at least a few really new things in educational philanthropy. One is the privately endowed university founded by a single large fortune. Another is the similarly endowed nonteaching educational foundation.

The more detailed description of the philanthropy of this period brought out the fact that among the old colonial foundations, as well as among colleges founded in the early national period, State aid was entirely lacking, while gifts were greatly increased both in numbers and size. It was noted that among the old colonial colleges the percentage of conditional gifts increased, while gifts to permanent funds showed a slight relative decline. 111512 22- In the colleges of the early national period almost the opposite tendency was Bhown rapid growth of permanent funds and rapid increase In gifts to the general fund, in Mil the colleges professorships, scholarships, and llbrarj were well remembered, though L r ifts to libraries among the older colleges did nol grow so rapidly; is was true in the yonnger schools. Everywhere it ii. is Ip."cii the fashion t" iri t the college" outright or toward some main feature like buildings, equipment, library, professorships, or scholarships. As compared with other kinds of philanthropy the data show that higher education is 01 f the greatest recipients of charity we have to-day, that a vast permanent endowment for higher education is being bnili op, and that philanthropy still hears the larger portion of the entire burden of cost. They bring out chariy the recent large movement of philanthropy toward the development of professional and technical schools and women's colleges, and also toward the larger support of church hoards of education, the functions of which have been much enlarged in recent years.

GREAT EDUCATIONAL FOUNDATIONS.

During the last portion of the present period the greal private foundation appeared a- a form oj educational philanthropy which was practically new Bach of these foundations represented the ideas ami aspirations of the one man whose fortune trave ji existence. Dominated by no church or religious creed, ami not even by the man who established it. but only by public opinion ami the corporation laws of State and Nation, these foundations have en tered the educational held ami left an Impress on practically every type of educational enterprise in the country, whether private. Slate, or church.

The whole business and financial aspect of higher education has been studied and ill a sense made over as;1 result of the operations of these gifts, The college curriculum lias been more clearly differentiated from that of the ondary school, and standards of achievement in studies more clearly de fined. Attention has been forcefully called i the problem of the distribution of colleges and to the principles which should guide us In locating new col leges. Millions have been added to the general endowment of higher education Medical, legal, and engineering education have been enormouslj profited bj ll lear and Impartial studies that have been made of the-. gel Is and by financial assistance. The scientific studj of education has nol onlj been greatlj stimulated, bul contributions have 1 a made through experiments and investigation. The bounds of knowledge have been pushed out In oianj directions by extensive and costlj research. The principles involved in pen Bions for teachers have been thoroughly studied from ever angle and broadlj and with some measure of Satisfaction established.

Some doubtfl and teals and mnnv sharp criticisms have heen voiced le-l these powerful corporation might Bees to bin education and public opinion m favor oi wrong social, political, or business ideal This should be looked upon a n of health. Dei rain soclet) wusl uol be expected to take I,-in- on faith Even it there la a grain of danger from Buch cor Hrn h danger should be mercilesslj weeded out in seeking tor such ilai however, vve must not close our eyes to i bvious benefits which have ami must continue to accrue to higher education from these Bources, While ucletj must Insist upon it right to control such corporations, it must,, oi he blind i" the difficulties these foundations have had to lace iii blazii the new trails which thej resyectlvelj have chosen to mark out In the Held of higher education. If the church, the State, the university, the professor, and the general public will continue to distinguish between Intelligent criticism, on the one hand, and mere suspicion and gossip on the other, and remember that a wise administration of these gifts is largely dependent upon a cooperating and appreciative beneticiary, then this, the greatest experiment in educational philanthropy that has ever been tried, will continue to prove its worth to society.

DEVELOPMENTS BEARING UPON A THEORY OF ENDOWMENTS.

From all this giving, what have we learned about the meaning of philanthropy itself? What attitude shall the State, the church, and society in general take toward the great stream of gifts that is continuously pouring into the lap of higher education in the country?

It is obvious that gifts to colleges are accepted by all as great blessings, and practically nowhere is there evidence that people fear the power which may some day be exercised through these gifts; that is how firmly the college has established itself in the confidence of the people. So many thousands of people have contributed small or large gifts to build these schools, so closely have the schools been associated with the church, and so intimately have they woven themselves into the life of the people that they are everywhere fully trusted, and thus far no very bad effects of philanthropy have been felt. 2 Even the great privately endowed institutions like Cornell (accepted with much misgiving at the outset in many quarters) have now fully won the confidence of the people in general, of the church, and of the State. This is not surprising in the light of the study of the conditions placed upon the thousands of gifts classified in the course of this study.

If there is any misgiving in the minds of the people about any educational philanthropy to-day, it is perhaps in reference to one or another of the recently established nontea'ching foundations. Here some uncertainty exists, as has been pointed out, though even here there is comparatively little that has not been accepted in most quarters with full confidence.

If philanthropy has so nearly won the entire confidence of the people, it is because of the record philanthropy has made for itself. In defining the meaning of education, or in setting the limits to its participation in college building, donors have not departed too far from the accepted ideas, ideals, and practices of the time and of the people they sought to serve. Millions have been given for permanent endowment but the practice has been to endow "the college," a "professorship,"' a "scholarship," a given line of "research," a "library," and rarely or never to define with any severe detail just what is to be included under the term "college," "professorship." "scholarship," etc. The result is that the writer has found little evidence of harmful or even useless foundations, large or small.

In the light of these facts it seems fair to assume that the great dominating motive in educational philanthropy has been desire to serve society: or, if we prefer, desire for a very high type of notoriety. So far as social progress is concerned, these are but two views of the same thing.

2 The writer did not find it feasible in this study to inquire into the number of gifts that have really laid a burden upon the college. In his autobiography, President White, of Cornell, expresses the opinion that our colleges have too frequently been

the recipients of such gifts as an observatory, leaving thfi college the responsibility of purchasing instruments and caring for upkeep.

It has been pointed out that most that lias been done toward developing n theorj of educational philanthropy in this country has grown directly ut of the practice rather than nt of the studies of social and political theory. The country lias faced and BOlved certain Fundamental questions as they have arisen, as: The function of the State in higher education; the Function of the church in higher education; the Function of private philanthropy in teaching and Don teaching activities touching higher education. In settling these questions there has heen endless debate and some bitterness of feeling, yd we have Fully ac-ee ted the idea of state endowed higher education, and, according to our practice, defined that education in the broadest possible way. This acceptance o State-endowed education did not rule out the church, whose activities in colli building are as much appreciated and as well supported as ever. Thai there

Should have heen a clash between the old idea of church-directed education and the new idea of State education was to lie expected. The outcome of uch a lash in this country, however, could not have been different from what it was. Similarly, there was a clash between the church and the privately endowed types of colleges, but each has a well-established place in present practice.

In this country we have not confined ourselves to any single notion about who shall bear the burden of higher education. The State establishes a uni vcrsity but it also encourages the work of the church and of private philanthropy." The practice is therefore based npoU a theor. v that is not fully in lme witii those of the early English, French, and German philosophers. It is far more liberal, being based rather upon the underlying conceptions of our social ami political organization.

Ownership of property in this country carries with it the right of bequest, and the "'dead hand" rests, in some decree, upon most of the institutions of higher education. We fully respecl the rights and the expressed wishes of thi educational benefactors but this Btud) shows that the benefactors base also respected the rights of society, not the society of today only but that of inline generations us well. There has been a growing tendency for colle ami universities to study the terms of proffered benefaction with utmost care and to refuse to accept gifts to which undesirable conditions are attached similarly there luis been a growing tendency on the part of benefactors either to accept terms suggested by the institution or i make the glfl practice 11) without conditions or with Specific provision for future revision of the COOdl tlons named This, it seems to tin writer, mark- an achievement which guarantees society against most if not ail ii vile associated vviih endowed educal ion.

After an examination of the hundreds of documents which have Furnished the basis of tin- study, the writer is Inclined to look upon educational philan tinopv as an essentia and highly important characteristic democracy.

ii a statement were made of the theorj which has been evolved or the principles which have heen arrived at in the almost three centuries of prac lice, the) would seelll In be BSOUt as follows: iii permanent endowment of higher education bj the state, bj the church, or other association, or bj Individuals! Is desirable.

(2) All U'ift I" education, whether for present Use or f,, r permanent en rlowment, whether large or-mall, should be encouraged, because the) open nillv,,- p ' mail.-ntlr.-lv.,. r lit CStt " I l ftM fr,. ii.

. Imvv 4 As in. It- t In-. i r. i r. J I up large possibilities in the way of educational investigation and experiment and because the donor is brought into an intimate relationship with an enterprise that is fundamental to the national life.

(3) The wishes of a donor as expressed in the conditions of his gift shall be respected and fully protected by the State.

(4) It is desirable that the conditions controlling a gift shall be stated in general terms only, and that the methods of carrying out the purposes of the donor be left largely to the recipient of the gift.

(5) Finally, it is desirable that even the purpose of a gift should be made alterable after a reasonable period of time has elapsed, and, if it be desirable, that the gift be terminated.

Lightning Source UK Ltd.
Milton Keynes UK
17 July 2010
157101UK00001B/39/P

9 781152 686243